Sainsbury's Homebase Guide to

FRUIT GARDENING

David Stuart

CONTENTS

NOTES
For convenience, ease of growing symbols have been incorporated in the A — Z sections.
They can be interpreted as follows:
   *Easy to grow fruit
  **Fruit which require more than average care
***Temperamental or difficult to grow fruit
These symbols are appropriate provided the soil is
suitable and fertile.

Published exclusively for
J Sainsbury plc
Stamford Street, London SE1 9LL
by Cathay Books
59 Grosvenor Street, London W1

First published 1984

© Cathay Books 1984
ISBN 0 86178 259 3

Printed in Hong Kong

INTRODUCTION

There is no reason why even the tiniest garden should not produce some sort of fruit for its owner. Most of the major crops are fairly adaptable in their demands, both for the available space and for the gardener's time. Some of the less usual fruits grow happily in deep shade, or on peaty soils, in very cold gardens, in pots on the patio or terrace, in sun-rooms and greenhouses, in conservatories or even on a moderately sunny windowsill or protected balcony.

FRUIT TREES

Most of the tree fruits (commonly called 'top fruits') will still crop heavily even when they have been grafted on to dwarfing stocks and kept heavily pruned. Against a house or garden wall or a substantial fence, it is not at all difficult to grow apples and pears. Apricots, cherries, plums, figs, nectarines, peaches, even vines, mulberries, filberts, quinces and almonds will flourish if given a little extra attention; likewise the humble gooseberry and redcurrant.

Since apples and pears can be heavily pruned to reduce them to a single branch, in which state they are called 'cordons', even a minute garden can contain as large a collection of types of each fruit as a whole orchard. Alternatively, it is possible to buy apple or pear trees which have several sorts of fruit grafted to the same trunk. 'Family trees', as they are known, can yield a selection of lovely fruits throughout the season.

To some eyes, the sorts of fruit that have been trained are never as beautiful as trees allowed to go their own way, but in spring most of them can rival any of the shrubs commonly grown against walls, and excel them in late summer or autumn as fans, espaliers and cordons laden with ripening fruit in a marvellous range of colours.

While in most gardens the shelter and warmth provided by a wall is essential for the choicer fruits like nectarines, peaches and vines, some top fruit will produce abundantly when trained along free-standing frameworks of wires and posts. Grown in this way they form useful screens to enclose the kitchen garden or disguise the unsightly view of a shed or compost heap. Such screens can also be used to make a backdrop for herbaceous borders, where their neat formality contrasts splendidly with the colourful luxuriance of the border itself. Old kitchen gardens often used to have the central path flanked with flower and herb borders, backed by neatly pruned apples and pears. Most of the lovely borders have vanished now, but often ancient fruit trees remain.

Owners of moderately sized gardens often take immense trouble to plant decorative trees that provide focal points for the design or a 'specimen' tree to enhance the lawn. There are few purely decorative trees that can challenge the beauty of the flowers of a mature pear or cherry, or boast a perfume more entrancing than that of the apple. None is more stately than a full-grown walnut, or more picturesque than a mulberry or medlar. The medlar, too, has dramatic autumn foliage, and the golden colour of quinces or profusion of elderberries are hard to beat.

SOFT FRUITS

The bush fruits (usually called 'soft fruits') can also be grown in small gardens, and many can be put to decorative use. Some can be trained against walls or wire frames in the same way as the top fruits. Red and white currants make excellent cordons; blackcurrants are only slightly more difficult to manage. Although none of them bears pretty flowers, the plants look lovely when they are hung with strings of shiny and translucent berries.

Gooseberries are also easily trained to walls, and it is possible to find varieties that have amber, yellow, scarlet or purple berries. They also make excellent hedges, and were often used in this way in old kitchen and cottage gardens. Once they have reached a certain age, the bushes will need thinning out every year, while remaining productive and decorative. They make useful windbreaks that in-

Grapes ripening on a mature vine

4

crease the productivity of the whole garden. They do need some sort of protection from birds (see page 21).

Some of the other soft fruits can make attractive screens if attached to a wire framework (for construction, see page 12). The easiest fruits to use in this way are the blackberry and its allies. For decorative screens, the elegant parsley-leafed blackberry is a good choice; for screens that are also to have a defensive use, the prickly 'Himalaya' variety is highly effective.

GROWING FRUIT IN POTS

You can grow your own fruit even if you have a garden with no soil at all, because many tree fruits and some bush ones will flourish in pots as long as they are in a good quality soil-based compost and kept well watered. Obviously, the larger the pot the larger the tree it can support, and the more fruit you will have. Apples, pears, peaches, cherries and especially figs all do well. A 30 cm (12 in) pot should allow a 1.2-1.5 m (4-5 ft) tree.

Potted fruit trees look very pretty and even if you have a good-sized garden (and a greenhouse or sun-room), they are useful as they can be forced under glass and returned outdoors once the crop has been picked.

It is not advisable to grow soft fruit in pots, for the yield does not justify the trouble taken. The exception is the strawberry, which does well in pots, and is easily forced to give an early though small crop.

Most of the subtropical (or Mediterranean) fruits also do well in pots and the citrus fruits make extremely handsome plants, if sometimes difficult to manage. Lemons and tangerines are probably the best; most of the others need to be planted directly into the greenhouse beds, or in large tubs. Useful crops are easily obtained, though it is important to buy a commercial stock if you can since seedlings can take up to fifteen years to bear fruit which even then is not succulent enough to repay your patience.

If you can provide enough warmth under glass, or have some well-made frames, melons repay a lot of work by providing very good fruit. Pineapples, too, can give delicious fruit, and were once grown as quite a common crop in British greenhouses.

FRUITS FOR GROWING IN SHADE

A north-facing garden, or one shaded by the house or other buildings, can still produce delicious fruit, of which morello cherries are perhaps the most sumptuous. Sometimes described as 'bitter' cherries, to distinguish them from the 'sweet' sorts, morellos are not especially sour. They are usually recommended for cooking, for which purpose they are splendid, but many gourmets find a dish of dark red juicy morellos a more delicious end to a meal than any of the dessert types.

Quinces grow well in shade and appreciate a damp situation even more. The fruit must be cooked before eating – the Elizabethans liked them roasted but a dishful of the speckled greeny-gold fruits smells so marvellous and looks so beautiful that it may take some while before they reach the stove.

Fresh nuts have an interesting flavour and texture; a relation of the hazelnut, filberts are also happy in shade, and are well worth growing. The male catkins are attractive in spring, and the different varieties will provide a range of colours, from greenish yellow to scarlet. The foliage is good all summer.

Raspberries and strawberries are both, in their natural state, woodland plants, and will give you a crop without much direct sunlight. Try growing the little alpine strawberries, rather than the fat modern hybrids which need sun to develop their fullest flavour. Alpines have a lovely flavour and bear fruit throughout the summer.

North-facing walls or shaded gardens can also produce quite good currant fruits. Red and blackcurrants were commonly grown in the shaded parts of the lovely walled kitchen gardens of Georgian Britain. In these conditions, the plants ripened much later than those in the sun, and so lengthened the time when their fruit was available. Gooseberries, excluding the dessert types, will also survive in shade.

Fruits can also be used to provide garden shade. While few northern gardeners often feel that need, in the southern parts of the country a shady part of the garden is essential for summer afternoons. While standard fruit trees offer the most pleasant shade, in a very limited space, an arbour or pergola is a better alternative. Vines are easily trained over such

a structure and cast a romantic shadow. With a good summer, and an early maturing variety, you should have a good crop just as the evenings become cooler.

FRUITS FOR GROUND COVER

Most gardeners today are busy people, interested in low-maintenance gardening and ground-cover plants. Two fruits that fall into these groups and which suppress weeds are rhubarb and strawberries. If the thought of a large area of ordinary rhubarb is unappealing, use *R. palmatum*, which has marvellously frilled leaves, or plant the red-leafed variant of the ordinary rhubarb.

Alpine strawberries are better than hybrids for ground-cover. Runnering ones can be slightly too invasive, though they are easily removed when they get out of hand. Many interesting forms exist, some with variously coloured and shaped fruit. The white-fruited one has an exquisite flavour.

CHOOSING THE BEST VARIETIES

All the major fruit crops have been grown for thousands of years. Because most of them are also commercially very important, there are immense numbers of varieties in existence. For gardeners planting fruit for the first time, the choice of types is bewildering. Many simply plant varieties that they know from the greengrocer, or see at the local garden centre.

The exquisite, and delicious, strawberry fruit

Top fruits are going to be in your garden for a long time. If you are not sure what to plant, do some research. First, have a look at local gardens, nurseries or garden centres, and see what they grow. If possible taste the produce of what you find. There are often old and local varieties which are particularly suited to your conditions. Second, look for specialist fruit nurseries. Many of them carry stock of less usual varieties which, while they may not suit the commercial growers, may provide good eating for the private gardener. You may also be growing an ancient fruit variety that is part of the gardening heritage. A 'new' variety may be larger, brighter and glossier, but will not necessarily taste better than the old.

HOW MUCH WORK IS INVOLVED?

All fruits need a certain amount of attention. Lots of other creatures like fruit as much as human beings do, so the crop needs careful protection. Furthermore, highly developed fruit species need pruning at least once a year if they are not to become a barren tangle. The task is not difficult. If the plants are few in number the work will not be arduous. If you plant a lot of fruit, however, you will have to devote a greater amount of time to them as they mature. The pleasure of eating your own fruit will be an ample reward.

BASIC PRINCIPLES

Once you have decided that you would like to grow fruit in the garden, take a closer look at the sites you can offer the plants. While many garden flowers will give plenty of colour despite conditions which do not really suit them, many fruits, to give of their best in terms of yield and flavour, need the best conditions the gardener can provide. This is particularly true of top fruit, for not only are the plants more expensive to buy than those of the soft fruits, but you will also be working with them for many years and they occupy a large amount of space. They must justify their presence by successful crops. Most fruits like full sunlight, summer warmth, shelter from winds and adequate rainfall. Optimum conditions like these can sometimes be created by the gardener even in locations that are apparently unfavourable.

Every garden has an individual character as well as being subject to regional influences. For example, it might be near the sea and enjoy mild winters, or bask in a sheltered valley on a south-facing slope. On the other hand, a seemingly ideal garden may be in heavy shade from nearby trees at certain times, be turned into a wind tunnel by nearby buildings, or be in a frost pocket. It is important to take such features into account when planning the fruit garden.

VARIATIONS IN CLIMATE

All gardeners, whether in Sussex, Yorkshire, or Ross and Cromarty should remember that local climate is far more important than mere latitude. For example, there are gardens in coastal parts of Scotland which will produce splendid crops of peaches, apricots and figs from wall-trained trees, yet a dozen miles inland even quince trees, reputed to be hardy, can be killed by the cold.

One of the best ways of finding out what will grow well in your area is to look at neighbouring gardens, to contact – or, better still, join – a local gardening society, ask at your local nursery or contact the nearest college of agriculture. You will discover which varieties and which crops do especially well in

your area. It is best to seek local advice before ordering from a catalogue or buying from a garden centre. Supplement the information you get from books with other people's experience of actual conditions.

Whatever your location, however windy and cold, do not despair. There are excellent apple and pear varieties that will bear fruit in the coldest gardens; even wet mountain hillsides can provide blueberries, strawberries, raspberries and rowans.

FRUITS SUITABLE FOR GROWING AGAINST WALLS

south-facing wall: peaches, nectarines, figs, apricots (in the North), greengages, the best sorts of apple and pear (in the North).

east-facing wall: sweet cherry, apples, pears, plums, greengages, damsons, quince, all soft fruit.

west-facing wall: apricots (in the South), mulberry, sweet cherry, apples, pears, plums, greengages, damsons, quince, all soft fruit.

north-facing wall: morello cherry, filberts, quince, some old varieties of apple and pear, most soft fruit (all these will do even better on other walls.)

THE IMPORTANCE OF LIGHT

All green plants need light to turn the simple nutrients which they can absorb through their leaves and roots into the complex substances needed to grow and reproduce. Almost every species mentioned in these pages needs as much sunlight as they can get to produce flowers and set fruit. In open countryside or in a large garden, there is no difficulty in providing plenty of light for your fruits. In a small garden, especially in a town, it can be more of a problem. Check your garden carefully at different times of the day. You may discover that a south-facing wall against which you were planning to grow some delicacy is actually shaded by something else most of the time. On the other hand, a north-facing wall may be useful if it still gets plenty of indirect light. If you do have good conditions, say a tall, sheltered and unshaded south-facing wall, use it to full advantage by growing a fine fruit like nectarine rather than an unfussy species like redcurrant.

WARMTH

In general, warmth is closely related to the amount of light available and is more important to young plants that are still growing than to established, mature specimens. Most fruits, even peaches and vines, though they will survive the winter in any part of Britain, may have insufficient warmth during the summer to ripen the fruit and new wood. Many fruits, including apples and cherries, need a cold period to trigger flowering in the following season; others such as apricots and green-gages, are particularly suited to a continental type of climate, with harsh winters and long hot summers.

If you live in one of the cooler parts of the country, choose early-ripening varieties, especially of apples, pears and plums, to give them as long as possible to reach perfection.

It is of course possible to modify temperature in various ways, especially for fruits grown against walls, though few modern gardeners will be keen to resort to the old method that involved heating the walls them-

selves. Old kitchen gardens often have walls with flues running through them, in which fires were lit to ripen late fruit and wood. There is another old method, however, which is still worth trying. In the eighteenth century, light wooden frames covered in oiled paper were hung from the top of a wall to the ground, making a mobile lean-to. Using polythene sheeting instead of paper, such screens are very useful in spring for peaches and apricots when late frosts or bad weather threaten to damage young fruitlets; they can be used again in late summer to ripen late varieties. If netting is stretched across the screens instead of polythene sheeting, they make a most effective means for protecting the crop from birds.

Greenhouses, either lean-to or freestanding, are the perfect structures for growing the most valuable garden fruits, and can allow you to produce good crops of peaches, nectarines, grapes, melons and figs. An unheated greenhouse is fine for all but subtropical fruit, or for the grandest sorts of fig and vine. This is true even for most of the north of England and Scotland. Even in the bleakest districts, only a slight heat in spring will be necessary.

Unheated frames, useful in small gardens,

Light wooden frames can be hung from a wall to protect the fruit either from unfavourable weather, using polythene sheeting or from birds, using netting stretched across the screens

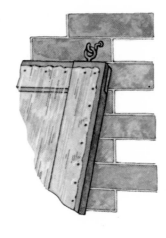

can be successfully used for strawberries or melons or both. It is possible to set out mature strawberry plants in the frames in late autumn, get a very early crop from the following season and then replace them with young melon plants.

Plants grown under glass enjoy warmth and shelter, but in the open, even against a south-facing wall, wind can greatly reduce the surface temperature. If the site is not naturally protected provide some shelter either from artificial windbreaks, or by planting wall shrubs and pruning them to form green buttresses.

Orchards of dwarf fruit bushes in exposed sites need artificial windbreaks, or the protection of hedges. Filberts are useful for this, and will give a respectable crop even when kept trimmed. Alternatively, use *Berberis vulgaris*, the common barberry – the berries of which are delicious as jam or candied – or the most upright growing gooseberry varieties, like 'New Giant', 'May Duke' or 'Langley Gage.'

It is not possible to grow the major top fruits in a frost hollow. In such a garden, late spring frosts will ruin flowers and fruitlets and cold autumn nights will arrive far too early. In this situation, content yourself with growing late-flowering and early-ripening varieties of soft fruit only, and provide as much protection for it as you can.

THE QUALITY OF THE SOIL

In general all the ancient outdoor crops will tolerate a wide variety of soils. They would not have survived if this was not so.

Unless your soil is permanently waterlogged or completely dry, there will be some fruits that will grow for you. Having said this, most species are ideally suited by deep loamy soil with a pH of about 6.5. Use a simple soil test kit to check the pH level of the soil in your garden. Soil which is too acid is often almost black in colour, and will register 5.5 or less. This can be corrected by adding hydrated lime in moderate quantities; if you overdo it, excess lime can remove nutrients from the soil. Alkaline soils, which may be either clayey or sandy, are often very pale in colour, but can be improved by adding peat.

Unless you have the ideal loamy soil, which is a nice brown, with a good crumbly struc-

ture, you will need to improve it by adding organic material, especially garden compost or well-rotted manure (horse manure is best if available). The addition of manure will be a frequent task in the cause of growing good fruit, as the plants will readily take up the nutrients it contains and need more.

Adding organic material also helps poor soil structures, whether they be yellow and gluey clay, or light and dry sandy soil. Peat can improve the structure of the soil, but it is low in nutrients, while organic manure keeps the nutrient level high, something that is difficult to check in a new garden. Some indication will be given by the weeds that are present. Chickweed is often a good guide: if there is plenty of it, and the leaves are large, crisp and juicy, nutrient levels are fine. If plants and leaves are small, or absent in an otherwise weedy garden, nutrient levels are low.

If the only organic material you can get is peat, use a general fertilizer as well, at the rate of 50-70 g/m^2 of ground (2-3 oz/yd^2). Granulated fertilizers are the easiest to handle.

Old inner city and new suburban gardens generally exhibit the worst characteristics. Inner city soil can be very acid and devoid of nutrients. Improve it by adding hydrated lime and as much well-rotted organic material as possible. Work the ground by growing vegetables for a few seasons. This will let you bring the soil up to standard, just on the acid side of neutral, and improve the structure and nutrient levels.

New gardens on old farm- or parkland can be quite good, as long as building work has not brought up subsoil, which is poor in nutrients, or put down brick and concrete rubble. If the weight of bulldozers and of other machinery has destroyed the soil structure, this will result in waterlogging and a hard level about 30 cm (1 ft) beneath the surface which is difficult to work. Restore structure and fertility by digging (double digging if necessary), and adding plenty of organic material.

Clear the garden of stones and rubble. All plants need to make a good root structure quickly in their early years, and cannot do it in a soil choked with obstructions.

Dampish soils will produce excellent quinces, pears if on quince stocks, plums, filberts and raspberries. Dryish soils suit many apples, peaches, nectarines and figs. Acid peaty soils will produce blueberries and cranberries, but little else. Really dry soils, especially those over chalk, can be very difficult. Add as much water-retaining material as possible, or even excavate suitably sized pits (say 1.5 cubic metres (50 cubic feet) for a dwarf top fruit), and fill them with imported top soil. Keep the plants well watered. Alternatively, grow fruit in tubs.

NATURAL AND ARTIFICIAL FERTILIZERS

Most of the soft fruits require a good diet. Apply garden compost, well-rotted manure or peat enriched with chemical fertilizer annually in winter. Strawberries, raspberries and redcurrants need extra potash. Apply 12 g/m^2 (½ oz/yd^2) before planting out. Other plants, which are happy with a nitrogenous diet need about a barrowload of compost for three or four square yards, which can be put down whenever you have time, though early spring is the most useful. Top fruits needing potash are apple and sweet cherry. Dress the soil in winter with potassium sulphate at 25 g/m^2 (1 oz/yd^2).

If you can not obtain manure, and do not have room to make a compost heap, feed the plants during the summer by watering them with suitable soluble fertilizers. Crops that need a diet rich in potash will like liquids of the type used for tomatoes. A general fertilizer will suit the rest.

Top fruits are worth cosseting for the first few years, while they are establishing themselves. Pears, plums, greengages, peaches and nectarines all benefit from good dressings of well-rotted manure or compost, while apples prefer potash.

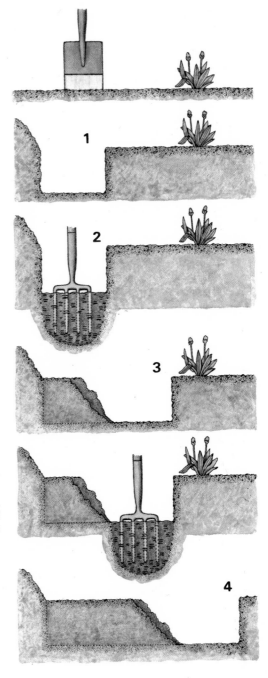

Double-digging. Start by digging a trench one spade's depth and 38 cm (15 ins) across (1). Loosen earth to a further spade's depth (2) and fork manure into the trench on top of loosened earth. Dig the next trench alongside in the same way and use the earth you take out to fill in the first trench (3). Proceed in this way until the last trench (4), which you fill in with earth from the first trench

11

ROUTINE CARE

The amount of trouble you take over planting, the first piece of work that you will have to do for your fruit, will affect most of your subsequent tasks. It is important, especially for top fruit, that the plant gets the best possible start in life so that even if you eventually have no time to devote to it you will still have a tree that will try to go on being productive. Fruit that gets a bad start may take years to get properly established, if indeed it ever does.

SUPPORTING TRAINED FRUITS

Top fruit and soft fruit grown as cordons, fans or espaliers need some sort of system to support them, whether free-standing or against a wall. The framework should be set up before the fruit is planted to avoid disturbing the bush or tree. What you need is a system of horizontal wires set about 30 cm (12 inches) apart. Use galvanized wire 2.5 mm (¹⁄₁₀th inch) in diameter for permanence. Against a wall, attach them to tensioning bolts with vine eyes set every 3.4 m (10 ft) along the length of the wires. In free-standing systems for fruit grown as screens or for espaliers in a fruit cage, the wires should be attached to strong timber posts. Use posts measuring 10×10 cm (4×4 inches) and treat them with fungicide. The end posts will need extra support at the base. Again, space the posts about 3.4 m (10 ft) apart.

PLANTING TOP FRUIT

If you have ordered plants from a distant nursery, they will arrive some time during the late autumn, or in winter, and will be bare-rooted; that is, most of the soil will have been shaken from their roots. Although most nurseries send out well-packed healthy material, open the package as soon as it arrives to check that the roots have not begun to dry out. If they have, soak the root ball in a bucketful of water for a couple of hours. Unlike stems, roots have no protection against drying out, and are easily killed by drought.

If you cannot plant immediately because

RIGHT: *Blueberries and vines, well-supported, growing in a protected orchard*

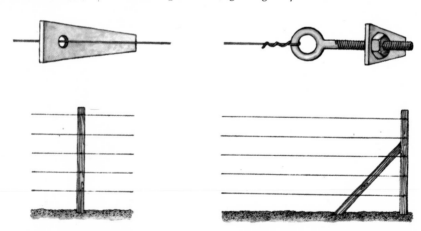

To support fruit, make a framework of horizontal wires threaded through vine eyes and attached to tensioning bolts
In a free-standing support system, attach the wires to strong timber posts with extra supports at the base of the end posts

the soil is frozen hard or sodden and too wet to work, the trees should be stored until planting is possible. Keep the plants in a shed, garage or cellar with the roots wrapped. Do not leave them outside to freeze. Do not leave the roots wrapped in a plastic sack; plastic does not provide enough warmth; and a long sojourn in plastic encourages rot. If the soil is fine for planting, but you do not have time to get the plants in the ground properly, simply dig a rough hole, put the roots in and cover them with enough soil to keep them firm. This process is known as 'heeling in'.

straw-filled will not do because it will be difficult to fill in between the tree roots.

Staking

All top fruits, whether bush or tree, need support for the first year or two, while the root system becomes strong enough to provide sufficient anchorage for the leafy top. It would be heartbreaking to find new standards bent or snapped off at the graft, or bushes half rocked out of the ground by a summer gale because they have not been staked.

Once you have excavated the planting hole and worked in some manure, place the stake

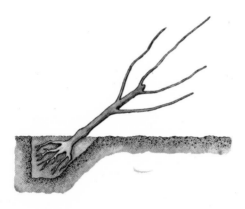

If you cannot plant immediately, the fruit tree should be 'heeled in'

When weather conditions permit and you have enough time, dig a hole at the chosen site that will comfortably hold the roots when they are well spread out. If you have to jiggle the plant around to get the roots to fit, it means that the hole is not large enough. The average hole will be 1 m (3 ft) across and 60 cm (2 ft) deep.

If possible, fork a bucketful or two of compost or well-rotted manure into the soil at the bottom of the hole. Do not use fresh manure as it contains active chemicals which will damage plant tissues. Failing these, use a good handful of bone-meal. Fork some bonemeal or fine-textured compost into the excavated soil. Coarse compost or rotten manure that is still

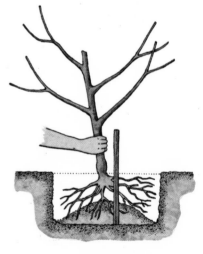

Put the stake in position first in the planting hole and then plant the tree with the roots well spread out (top). It can be useful to have a buffer to prevent the stake rubbing against the tree

in position. Square or round stakes are equally good, but they must be strong enough to do the job. Poles 7.5 cm (3 inches) in diameter or 7.5 ×7.5 cm (3×3 inches) stakes, will be sufficient for the average standard tree. The length of the support depends on the length of the plant's stem. The top of the stake, when driven into the base of the planting hole, should be just below the first branch of the standard. If the stake projects into the crown of the tree, branches will rub against it in the wind and lose their bark. Position the stake on the prevailing windward side of the tree, so that the tree generally pulls on the stake. On bushes, the stake inevitably stands among the branches. Secure a strong central branch as firmly to the stake as possible.

Filling in

Stand the young plant in the hole to ensure that the size is right. Spread the roots out evenly and with care. Neatly trim off any that are broken or damaged. Put a spadeful or two of excavated soil over the roots and shake the plant gently to settle the soil between the main roots. To get the planting level right, find the graft, which is usually visible as an oblique swollen ring on the stem and make sure that it is several inches above the soil level. Sometimes it is possible to see where the old soil level was when the plant was in the nursery bed, in which case simply plant to the same depth.

Shovel in some more soil, working it in carefully among the roots. Let the soil settle as you go, without leaving any air pockets that could fill with water or cause the tree to subside later. Firm down without ramming it in too hard. Continue until the hole is filled, and the tree firmly planted.

Secure the tree to the stake. Strips of cloth make good ties, or stout twine threaded through a piece of hosepipe. Do not use nylon string or twine because it is so sharp that it will cut into the bark. A buffer of some sort between the tree and stake is useful.

CONTAINER-GROWN TREES AND BUSHES

These can be bought and planted at any time of year, using exactly the same method as for bare-rooted trees. Open up the lowest part of

Fruit trees: distances between plants

Distances between plants depend on the vigour of the variety: plants of a non-vigorous variety should be spaced according to the smaller of the recommended figures

	APPLES		PEARS	
	space between plants	rows	space between plants	rows
Centre leader bush	semi-dwarfing rootstock 4-6m	4-6m		
	dwarfing rootstock 2-5m	3-6m	2-6m	4-6m
Espalier	4-6m	2m	3-6m	2m
Oblique cordon	1m	2m	1m	2m
Fan	4-6m		4-6m	
Standard	6-10m	6-10m	6-10m	6-10m

	PLUMS		CHERRIES	
	space between plants	rows	space between plants	rows
Centre leader bush	3-6m	4-6m	Sweet 5-8m Sour 4-6m	Sweet 5-8m Sour 4-6m
Fan	4-6m		Sweet 5-8m Sour 4-6m	Sour 4-6m
Standard	6-8m	6-8m	Sweet 7-12m	

the root ball as much as you can before planting, paying especial attention to the coil of roots that often forms at the bottom of the bag or pot.

Once planted, water the young tree or bush copiously over the whole root area. Keep a close watch on the plant in the following months, especially in hot weather. It will take at least a season before there are sufficient new roots to let the tree fend for itself.

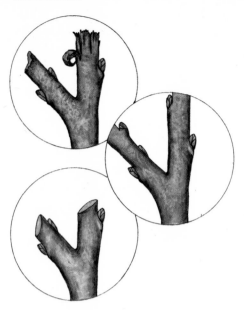

Use sharp secateurs to make clean, sloping cuts

PLANTING SOFT FRUITS

These are planted in the same way as top fruit. Bush soft fruits are small when sold, and do not need staking. Strawberries are planted into a prepared bed (see page 66).

PRUNING

Pruning ensures that the tree or bush is kept within bounds, furnishes a supply of fruiting wood, and allows light and air to reach the ripening fruit. The method of pruning varies from species to species, and depends also on the form of plant required.

Almost every tree and bush fruit that we are dealing with produces flowers along shoots that were formed the previous season (second-year wood). In some fruits (group 1) that second-year wood will not go on to produce flowers in the third year (e.g. morello cherries, peaches). In other cases (group 2), flower buds continue to form in subsequent years, often on short side shoots called 'spurs'. Most apples and pears, plums and sweet

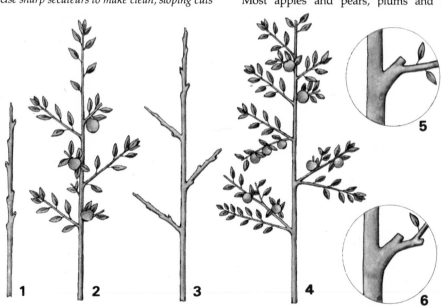

Group 1 (replacement shoot fruits). (1): Winter 1, fruit and growth buds along last summer's shoot. (2): Summer 1, prune shoots next to fruits to 2 or 3 leaves. Allow some shoots to grow for next year's fruit. (3): Winter 2, as winter 1. (4): Summer 2, as summer 1, but allow 5-6 leaves beyond last fruit on each branch. Pinch out side growths to 2-3 leaves except for one near the base. Allow this to grow as replacement for fruiting shoot. (5): Summer 2, after harvest, cut out shoot at junction with replacement. (6): Summer 3

cherries fall into this group.

It is nevertheless useful to think in terms of the spur when treating the first group of fruit types, where pruning has to ensure a constant supply of new wood. In general, this replacement wood can be thought of as very long spurs. 'Long spur' fruit includes raspberries and blackberries, vine, peaches and nectarines.

Be ruthless when pruning and thinning. All fruits, when grown in pruned forms, can be ruined if treated too tenderly. Allow only as much growth as you need to fill up the space available, or to give you fruit next year. Any more is superfluous. In some crops, such as vines, pruning needs to be carried out throughout the season; for others, it must be carried out once or twice a year.

FRUIT FORMS
It is very important to understand what the basic differences are between the various forms of fruit tree that are available (see also illustration of fruit forms, page 18).

Maiden
A single shoot, usually one year's growth after grafting. If you have sufficient self-confidence to go on to produce the other forms of tree from a maiden, and the time to wait an extra year or two for a crop, you can take advantage of the fact that maidens are cheap to buy and very easy to establish in the garden. Pruning for the various forms takes place in winter.

Cordon
A cordon is simply a maiden with side growths pruned back to form spurs. Some soft fruits, particularly redcurrants and gooseberries, make good cordons, but these forms are most often used for the majority of apple and pear varieties, which easily form short spurs. They can be grown on wire frameworks, or against walls. They are often trained to grow at an angle to give a greater length of stem and still be easily harvested. The word is also used for double or triple arrangements of branches.

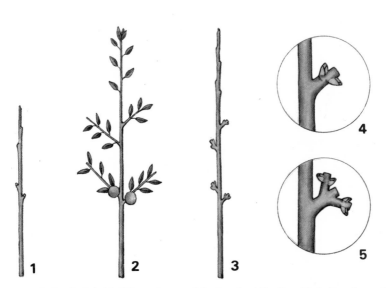

Group 2 (spur-producing fruits). (1): Winter 1, growth buds only at the tip with fruit and growth buds mostly at the base of last summer's growth. (2): Summer 1, prune side shoots so that 4-6 leaves remain. (3): Winter 2, prune side shoots to leave 2 buds. Allow the leading shoot to grow unless the space is filled; if so treat the leading shoot as a spur and cut back. (4): Summer 2, let only one of the buds produce a growth shoot. (5): Winter 3, after summer and winter pruning a small spur is being built. After several more years this will need radical shortening

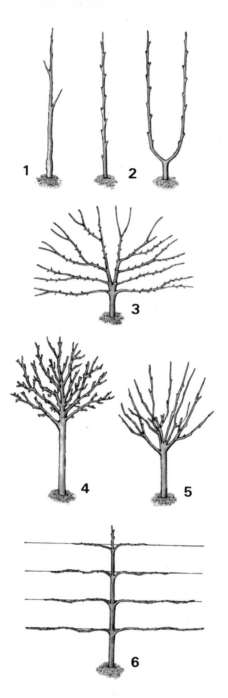

Fans

Trees of fan shape are always grown against a wall or supporting framework. The maiden is cut back to 20-30 cm (8-12 inches), and the two uppermost shoots that then develop are allowed to grow. They are tied into wires or canes to keep them in one plane, and are then themselves cut back and allowed to sprout two new shoots. The resultant 'spokes' are kept in the same plane, and are also trained along canes to keep them neat and straight. Because fans take time and care to produce, they are expensive to buy.

Fans are suitable for vigorous types of fruit, especially plums, greengages, peaches, nectarines, mulberries, apricots, figs and morello cherries. However, apples and pears can make splendid-looking fans, and because the spurs are so short, the structure shows up well.

Standards and half-standards

All side growths are pruned away and the leader allowed to grow to the required height – 2 m (6 ft) and 1 m (3 ft) respectively. The growth point is then removed and the topmost three or four outward-facing branches that then develop are allowed to grow on.

Espalier

A well-trained and cared-for espalier looks marvellous in flower and fruit. They are more useful than fans, as they are easily trained to fill all available space. Each of the side branches can be extended as far as necessary. Because this is the most artificial of the pruned tree forms, it suits only obedient species, particularly apples and pears.

The maiden is cut back to just above the height of the first wire, generally 30 cm (12 inches) above ground level. Three new shoots are allowed to form; the uppermost is allowed to grow vertically; generally the other two are allowed to grow out at a wide angle, tied to canes to keep them straight, and carefully lowered to the horizontal in autumn.

The following season, the vertical shoot is again cut back, this time to the level of the second wire, and so on for as many subsequent years as there are wires.

It is very tempting, having planted a nice tall maiden, not to cut back in the hope that sufficiently vigorous side shoots will grow out

A maiden (1); single and double cordons (2); a fan (3); a standard (4); a bush (5) and an espalier (6)

18

where required. Though they can be encouraged to do this by making a nick in the bark just above each bud that you need to turn into a branch, this is rarely satisfactory.

Bushes

These vary in shape, both according to the natural habit of the fruit variety concerned, but also to the needs of the gardener. Gooseberries and currants are most often grown in this way, but many of the top fruits are too. Their small size makes bushes very useful in small gardens, because they are easier to prune, protect, spray and harvest.

Most top fruit bushes are produced by shortening a maiden and letting a number of side shoots grow. 'Spindle' and 'Pyramid' bushes are both used for apple, and the second also for pears. Both keep the central leader shoot. In spindles, the side branches are tied or weighted down to keep them horizontal, like an espalier, but in three rather than two dimensions. In a pyramid, the branches are allowed to grow upwards.

With short-spur fruits, it is an easy matter to grow the main structure of the bush, and then encourage and prune spurs in exactly the same way as for an espalier or fan. For long-spur types, allow the bush to build up a structure, then remove fruited side shoots.

Soft fruit trees

These are naturally small and seldom outgrow their allotted space. Gooseberries, redcurrants and whitecurrants, which can be made to spur, are best treated in the same way as bush apples. When the main branches and the spurs become too congested, cut one or two branches out each year. Of the new shoots that grow as replacements, select the strongest and remove the others.

Blackcurrants should be cut to within 2.5 - 5 cm (1-2 inches) of the ground just after planting. The prunings can be used as cuttings to raise new plants. No further pruning should be necessary until the bush is several years old when, after harvesting, you should cut out between one quarter and one third of the branches at near ground level. This will encourage plenty of new growth, while keeping the bush open enough to ripen both fruit and new wood.

WHEN TO PRUNE

Most pruning takes place in winter. It is a pleasant garden task on a sunny day in December or January. Remember that fruit against a wall will begin to grow as soon as the sunlight begins to gain strength. Get all pruning done before winter spraying starts, and well before there is the slightest sign of the buds expanding. Chemicals used at that time will harm green tissue.

Do not prune plums, damsons, greengages or cherries in winter, as this can allow the entry of silver leaf infection. (Other sorts of tree are immune.) Leave them to late July or August when you are dealing with other plants that need summer pruning.

DWARFING STOCKS

Most top fruits are sold in a grafted form, since this method of propagation ensures constant characters for each variety. While it is possible to grow apples, pears and a number of others from cuttings, the resultant plants are often exceptionally vigorous.

Grafting is an ancient art. Before the Romans practised it, it was known that stock and scion need not be of the same species to make a satisfactory union, and that the type of stock used affected the growth habit of the tree it supported. Over the ages, the selection of stocks became increasingly refined. Today, it is possible to buy most fruits on stocks that dwarf them to varying degrees.

Stock and scion

When you buy a fruit tree, you are actually buying two plants, and you need to know what both of them are. If you have a small garden, and want bushes that remain in scale with it, check that the stocks will give you maximum dwarfing. If you want to make fans or espaliers, ensure that the stocks are only medium dwarfing. Orchard bushes need something less dwarfing still.

Most of the stocks, particularly for apples and pears, are known simply by code names. New sorts appear from time to time, so check with your supplier. Currently, M9 is the most strongly dwarfing stock for apples, followed by M26; M7 and MM 106 are semi-dwarfing. Pears are usually on Quince C (moderately dwarfing), or Quince A (semi-vigorous). Plums and their allies are usually on the semi-dwarfing St. Julien A, though orchard trees may be on Myrobalan B. Sweet cherries are semi-vigorous on Colt, or vigorous on Malling F 12/1.

POLLINATION

Most fruits need pollination to take place before the crop can develop. The task is generally performed by bees, but for greenhouse crops you will need to do it by hand (see below). You will also need to do it for certain fruits, such as apricots and greengages, planted against walls. In most seasons they will be in flower before the bees are about.

Hand pollination is an annual operation;

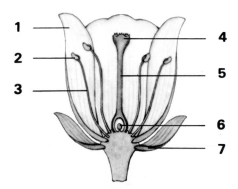

The different parts of a flower showing the petal or corolla (1), the anther (2) and filament (3) together forming the stamen, the stigma (4), style (5) and ovary (6) and the sepals (7)

however, other aspects of pollination need to be considered when planting many outdoor fruits. In many cases it is sufficient if pollen from one flower, or from other flowers on the same plant, is transferred to the stigma. Fruit formation ensues. Such plants are called 'self-fertile', and in the garden a single plant will produce a crop.

Other fruits, called 'self-sterile', can only be pollinated by pollen from a plant of another variety. To ensure a crop, two trees of different varieties, but which flower at the same time, must be grown.

Apples, pears, plums and sweet cherries have varieties which flower at different times in the spring. If you plant an early and a late sort, cross-pollination may not result because the flowers of one have faded before those of the other have opened. Varieties of these crops have therefore been split into groups, all members of which flower at the same time.

If possible, plant trees from the same group. The time of flowering is not related to ripening times, so you can still spread your crops over several weeks or even months.

Tables of cross-pollinating varieties are given in the entries for the main top fruits. The earliest and latest flowering groups have been omitted, because they do not contain well-known varieties. The list for each group is restricted to varieties which are easily obtainable, and have an excellent flavour.

Wall and greenhouse fruits

The shelter and warmth of a wall or glass encourage fruit trees to flower early. Apricots, greengages, peaches and nectarines and plums grown against a wall may all be in flower long before there are any bees around to pollinate them. You will have to do it yourself, using an artist's camelhair paintbrush. Buy the best you can afford for good results.

To see if the time is right, have a look at the anthers of the open flowers. It is easy to see if they have split open, revealing white or yellowish pollen. Dab the brush into each open flower you can find, transferring the pollen as you go. On a dry sunny day the brush should show the colour of the pollen.

Under glass, the same thing needs doing for peaches and nectarines. Strawberry plants being brought on early will need pollinating too, but it is usually sufficient to spray the flowers with water to distribute the pollen.

The flower trusses of vines need tapping gently to shake the pollen on to the stigmas, and thence in a yellow cloud to the ground.

Of the exotic fruits, only melons need special treatment. Their flowers are either male or female, most of them male. When the glasshouse is warm and dry, have a look at the boss of anthers in each male flower. If you can clearly see the powdery yellow pollen, pick the flower, strip away the petal tube, and push the boss into the female flower. Some gardeners like to leave the boss in position, but if there is plenty of pollen on it, this is not necessary.

FRUIT PROTECTION

Having erected a framework for the support of fruit, you will almost certainly need to provide another to protect it from birds. The easiest and most efficient solution to this problem is to buy a ready-made fruit cage, the extra expense of which will soon be defrayed by the increase in harvest. It is perfectly possible, however, to construct a fruit cage yourself. If you decide to do this, make it high enough to walk around comfortably inside – otherwise you will be bent double when trying to pick the fruit. Black plastic netting looks better than the bright green kind; galvanized wire netting, though long-lasting, is not necessarily the best choice, since rain washing off it can damage the plants beneath. Construct the cage so that the roof can be removed in the autumn, otherwise the first fall of heavy snow will make it collapse. It is usually worth having removable walls as well, so that the spring-time pollinating bees have free access to the flowers on the trees and bushes.

While fruit bushes are small, you can use the cage to grow strawberries too, moving them to a bed of their own when the bushes are established. Any fruit outside the cage can be protected with capacious cloches, using large hoops of wire threaded through a strip of netting. An alternative is to make a simple cage by driving 1.2 m (4 ft) posts into the ground and throwing sheets of netting over them. Top each post with a jam jar to stop netting getting caught on splinters. For larger areas, have long canes connecting the posts,

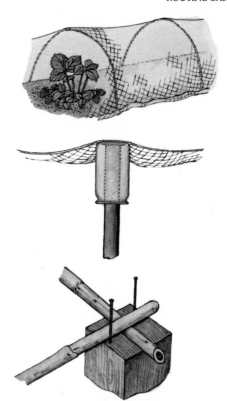

A cloche made with large hoops of wire (top). Top posts with a jam jar to protect netting (centre). Connect posts in a large cage with long canes (bottom)

securing them on top with two nails. Anchor the lower edge of the nets with hooks of galvanized wire. Neatly roll up any excess netting and secure it with more hooks. Do not let it get out of hand or birds will be caught up in it and injure themselves.

Do not try to protect your fruit by just throwing a piece of plastic netting over it. Not only will it be inadequate, since most birds will be cunning enough to find a way through, but when you remove it you are certain to damage the bush, since young shoots will grow through the net.

Wall fruit

Protective netting is useful for most fruits grown against a wall; it is essential for cherries and all soft fruits. It is easy to attach nets to the

21

topmost training wire. At the sides, either thread a tall cane through the netting, pushing the bottom of the cane into the soil at the base of the wall, or pin the netting to the wires on either side of the plant with wire hooks.

HARVESTING

The time of ripening depends on whether early or late varieties of a crop are used, where the plant is in the garden, and on the season. If there is room for several varieties, choose some that ripen at different times, to avoid having a dearth one month and a glut the next.

Most fruits need to be picked as soon as they are ripe. Currants can be left on the bush for a week or two after they have reached their full colour, provided they are protected from the birds.

Test pears and apples for ripeness by lifting each fruit gently from the branch in the palm of your hand. If it separates easily, harvest time has arrived. Remove the fruits carefully, as bruised or damaged specimens cannot be stored. If possible, harvest them into shallow baskets or boxes, and cart them down to the pantry or kitchen. They can be left for a day or two before wiping them clean and putting them into store.

STORING FRUIT

If possible, it is a good idea to have two places for storing fruit. One of these is only for the short term, for unripe fruit to ripen. A sunny shelf is best for melons, peaches and nectarines. Plums and greengages will ripen well enough on a kitchen shelf or in a pantry if you have one. A pantry is also useful for medlars and nuts, which will otherwise have to go in your long-term storage area.

A long-term storage place is necessary for winter varieties of apple and pear. It should be cool though frost-free, and humid. A cellar, shaded garage or shed or cool pantry is ideal. In old kitchen gardens, sheds on the north side of the north wall were often used for fruit storage. In small modern houses, a cupboard in a little-used room may suffice. Lofts, and the cupboard under the stairs, are usually so warm that the fruit will ripen too quickly.

Details on storing individual fruit species are given at the end of each entry.

GROWING FRUIT IN CONTAINERS

Fruits suitable for growing in containers include apples, cherries, figs, peaches, pears and citrus fruits. Use soil-based compost, since peat-based composts become much too compact in very large pots. Since they are also very light, they do not provide sufficient anchorage for plants of any size, and the wind will blow them over. If you use a John Innes compost, it will contain enough food for the first season's growth. In subsequent years, feed the plants weekly.

Earthenware pots are much better-looking than plastic ones – especially those with a fake antique finish – and are also heavier. While this has the advantage of giving anchor in wind, it also makes them more difficult to move around the garden or patio. Good garden centres should have 30 cm (12 inch) earthenware pots. Wooden tubs also make good-looking containers. Make sure that the wood has been treated against rot. In formal gardens, square Versailles tubs painted white are appropriate. The originals commonly had iron hooks on two sides, which could be looped over poles to make it easier to lift them. Some even had hinged sides so that the soil could be renewed *in situ*. Tubs made from half barrels are fine for informal settings, and will comfortably hold a cherry, peach or fig.

Whatever container you use, ensure that there are adequate drainage holes. No tree will grow in a waterlogged pot. Put at least 2.5-5 cm (1-2 inches) of pebbles or broken clay pots in the bottom. Replace at least some of the soil every two or three years. It is usually possible to take out the top layer and put back fresh soil, enriched with compost or well-rotted manure. If all the soil needs to be replaced, you will need to remove the plant from the container. This is easier with the pot or tub on its side, and with the soil fairly dry. Plant and soil will come out all of a piece. Gently poke or hose at least the outer soil from the mass of roots. Replant with care, keeping the root system intact. Eventually, the plant will outgrow the container, and you will have to start again with a new plant.

FORCING

If the pots or tubs you use are small enough to be portable, the fruits in them can be forced to

produce crops early in a greenhouse or sun-room. Since almost every fruit except the fig needs a cold period to trigger flowering, leave the pots outdoors for December and January. Then bring them into gentle warmth and wait for the flowers to appear. Pollinate the flowers by hand. Use self-pollinating varieties if you only want to force one or two pots. Once the fruit has ripened, put the plant

Citrus fruits grown in pots make attractive plants and can be taken indoors for protection or to force an early crop

outdoors again. Make the most of any spare space under glass at the end of the season to ripen off late-maturing varieties of fruit planted in pots, such as a cane or two of some of the grander grape varieties.

23

COMMON TROUBLES, PESTS AND DISEASES

UNFRUITFULNESS

If a fruit bush or tree which has been planted within the last couple of years displays plenty of healthy growth but no flower buds, one or more of the following factors may be in operation:

Maturity: Some young top fruits, especially if on vigorous stocks, may take several years to reach flowering size. Seedling trees, ungrafted, can take many years. If it is still possible, check which stock the scion is on. Otherwise, be patient.

Too much, or incorrect, feeding: Some types of apple, some soft fruits and most figs, will produce only leaves if they are fed heavily with nitrogenous manure. Stop mulching. If you are growing apples as bushes or standards with bare ground beneath, try sowing grass. This will compete for the available nitrogen, and reduce the speed of growth of the bushes on trees. Where possible, dress the soil with a potassium-rich fertilizer in winter.

Unproductive wall-fruit sometimes responds to root-pruning, as do small top fruit bushes, but this is a job for skilled gardeners only to tackle.

Incorrect pruning: Check your methods. Check also the variety of fruit you are growing. Some pears and apples are tip-bearers, with flower buds borne at the end of last season's growth. If your plants cannot now be identified by type, try not pruning for a year and see if the situation remedies itself.

Biennial bearing: Some apple varieties fruit so heavily that they only manage a crop every second season. Again, wait a year and see what happens.

If the plant is growing well, and there are plenty of flowers, but no fruit follows:

Early flowering: The plants may have been in flower very early, before there were any bees to effect pollination; this is most common in wall fruit. Next year, try hand pollination.

A bad season: This may be either because of late frosts, or a long wet spell at flowering time. If it can be done easily, try protecting plants from late frosts with netting, sacking or plastic sheeting draped over them.

No variety suitable for cross-pollination nearby: Check your variety for its pollination requirements.

If the plants are neither growing, flowering nor fruiting properly, but are fairly new and were planted with care, remember that it can take a season or two for the new trees to establish themselves, especially if you bought them bare-rooted. Do not forget to keep them well watered.

If neighbouring plants are also growing weakly, the nutrient levels in the soil may be low. Try manuring or adding a general fertilizer. If that makes no difference, it would be worth your while to have your soil analysed by your local College of Agriculture.

RENOVATING NEGLECTED FRUIT

If you have taken over a run-down garden, many of the fruit bushes and trees may have become unproductive. With soft fruits, it is often best to scrap the lot, purchasing new and virus-free material, and planting on another site – virus infections can be transferred from old soil.

If you are keen to keep some of the old soft fruit, try cutting blackcurrants to within a few inches of the ground in winter, and selecting the strongest of the new shoots the following summer, discarding the rest. Tangled gooseberries and redcurrants can be heavily pruned, again in winter, so that only the best main branches are left. The final structure should be as open as possible so that new growth is not crowded.

Old top fruits are more of a problem. If you have neglected espaliers, fans or cordons, try cutting back to the original form, even if this means removing large branches. Very neglected espaliers can even be cut back to the main upright, and new shoots that form subsequently can be trained along the old wires.

Less neglected wall fruits will probably only need their spurs thinning out. Do this in winter, cutting them back to within a few inches of the main structure. Heavily trimmed spurs will not flower in the subsequent season, so if you want some fruit, leave some of the old spurs to be dealt with the following winter.

On overgrown bushes or standards, the problems are more complex. It is fairly easy to thin out the branches to give a suitably open structure. After pruning, paint large areas of bare wood with commercially available wound paints to stop the wood rotting. Having said that, it is important to decide whether or not you can maintain the resultant plant. If you cannot, then it might be worth grubbing the tree out and planting a new one. On the other hand, mature fruit trees, highly productive or not, are very beautiful, and can contribute a great deal to the overall garden scene. They should not be discarded without careful thought.

This well-established apple tree is a fine example of the magnificent structure formed by a well-trained espalier

PESTS AND DISEASES

Like all garden plants, fruit crops are susceptible to disease and attractive to pests. The
likelihood of damage varies from year to year
and from garden to garden. Pests which
ravage your neighbour's fruit may not touch
yours, and vice versa.

If you take over an established garden it is
much better to wait and see what the situation
is, than to launch into a full-scale spraying
programme. If you are laying out a new
garden, or planting new fruits, it is better to
take basic preventive measures, than to spray
against problems which may not appear.

However, be vigilant. Pests and diseases,
by their nature, spread fast. Get to know your
plants and how they grow. In this way, you
will notice immediately when young leaves
become oddly wrinkled or curled, or fruits
spotted. Watch out for unusual bird or insect
activity, and try to find the cause. None of this
will be a chore for the fruit-lover. Try to check
all the plants once a week. Unless you insist
on show-quality fruit, you will find that a
fairly relaxed programme will still give you
ample fruit of excellent flavour, even if with an
occasional blemish.

BASIC CONTROL

Garden hygiene is the single most important
preventive measure. In autumn, always clear
away fallen leaves and ungathered fruit. Both
can act as overwintering sites for various
fungal diseases, and as shelters for insect
pests, slugs and snails. Try trapping minor
pests like woodlice and earwigs. Neither
justifies a chemical-based attack.

On apple trees, use sacking bands or strips
of corrugated cardboard on the trunk and
main branches to trap codling moth caterpillars. If the bands are in place by mid-July, the
caterpillars, having eaten all they need, mi-
grate down the stems looking for somewhere
to pupate. The sacking or cardboard will be a
suitable place, and you can burn it in the
autumn. Next year infestation should be less.

Deal with sawfly moths by trapping the
wingless females as they climb the trunk and
stems in winter or early spring to await
egg-laying time. Smear the bark with grease
specially produced for the purpose, or attach
grease bands to the main trunk.

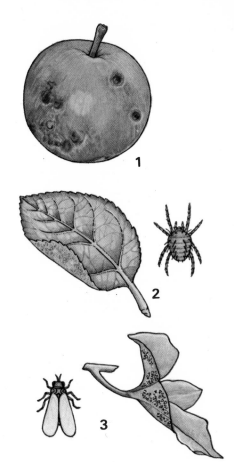

*Scab on a ripe apple (1), red spider mite and
infestation on an apple leaf (2), whitefly and
infestation on a melon leaf (3)*

BIRDS

It is difficult for the fruit-grower to have an
unqualified affection for birds. To keep them
off fruits that cannot be netted, use as many
bird scarers as you can think of – scarecrows,
model snakes (gardeners of old used to grow a
special variety of long, curly cucumber that
had the same effect), even model hawks on
strings. Glittering strips of metal foil can make
quite a noise in a light breeze, which might
deter the birds but in a small suburban
garden disturb your neighbours, too. Quieter
and much cheaper, are strips cut from a
compost or fertilizer bag. Make strips about

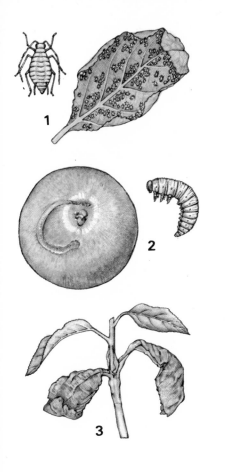

Aphid attack on an apple leaf (1), a sawfly maggot and its damage on an apple (2), peach leaf curl (3)

7.5 cm (3 inches) wide, and tie them on to strings stretched between canes 2.1 m (7 ft) high. After a gale, the string will be so twisted as to snap, but until then it will keep birds from gooseberries, plums, apples and alpine strawberries. Bottles rattling atop canes or small windmills sometimes work. All scarers need moving around every few days, or the birds become used to them.

CHEMICAL SPRAYS
Gardeners have been harvesting fruit from trees and bushes for hundreds of years, most of them without the assistance of chemical sprays. In modern conditions, however, it is difficult to dispense with some assistance against fungal disease and insect pests.

Systemic insecticides are absorbed by the plant and then distributed throughout its tissues. While this gives very good protection from pests and diseases, it does mean that the chemical cannot be washed off the fruit, and so systemics should never be used near harvest time. Always check the directions on the container. Some gardeners still prefer not to use them at all, and use only sprays that remain on the surface, and can be washed off.

When buying a spray, choose the largest one you can afford, bearing in mind its weight when full. Even if you have only a few moderate-sized fruit trees and some soft fruit, consider buying a knapsack sprayer. Ungainly and heavy when full, nevertheless they enable you to make a thorough job of spraying, without constantly having to refill the reservoir. Small handsprays are only really suitable for very limited outbreaks.

Watch the weather when spraying. Do not spray when it is windy or the tree will be unevenly treated and you may get spray on yourself, which can be dangerous. Do not spray when you know it is about to rain. Most chemicals need to dry on the plant.

It is important to spray plants at the right stage. Do not use winter tar oil after the buds have begun to expand. Do not use insecticides on plants in flower, or you will kill the bees. Even some fungicides can kill bees.

Some chemicals are very persistent. Always wash all fruits before eating or cooking. The labels on bottles or packets of chemicals should tell you how long they persist.

Remember that most insect pests are eaten by other insects as well, which is one of the reasons why the crop has survived down the ages. If you spray the pest and kill it, you'll also be killing the predators, so that the next pest will be able to invade unopposed. As in all things, moderation is the key.

Bud stages
Certain pests that attack fruit will only invade at a particular stage in the development of bud, flower or fruitlet. Spraying is effective at that stage only, and these are noted in the chart overleaf.

PEST	ON CROPS	DESCRIPTION	ACTION
APHIS (greenfly, blackfly, woolly aphis)	apple, plum and allies, pear, cherry, peaches, nectarines, currants, gooseberry, raspberry, strawberry		Numerous remedies. Malathion is effective. Pirimcarb and Permethrin are newer. Dimethoate is a good systemic type.
APPLE SAWFLY	Apples, sometimes crab apples	Adults not often seen. Maggots leave brown trails over first skin	Spray with BHC, Dimethoate or Fenitrothion just after petal fall.
BIG BUD MITE	Blackcurrants	Individuals minute. However, infected buds very swollen	Pick off affected buds. If problem gets worse next season, spray every 3 weeks with Benomyl.
CAPSID	Currants	Small jumping wedge-shaped insect in various colours	Dimethoate very effective. If you do not want to use a systemic, use Malathion.
CATERPILLARS	Apple, pear, plum and allies, cherry, apricot, gooseberry, currant		Bioresmethrin, Malathion, Trichlorphon all effective.
CODLING MOTH	Apples	Maggots found at apple core	Permethrin or Fenitrothion at petal fall, and again after 3 weeks.
GOOSEBERRY SAWFLY	Gooseberry only	Often feeding in groups at centre of bush	Malathion spray as soon as spotted.
RASPBERRY BEETLE	Blackberry, raspberry, loganberry	Grubs found inside harvested fruit	Malathion or Derris sprays. On raspberries as fruit colours, on blackberries when flowers open, on loganberries at end of flowering.
RED SPIDER	Apples, plum and allies, peach. Most fruit crops under glass	Individuals minute, reddish. Infested leaves pale, eventually withering. Short tips often covered with web	Hose frequently with water, or spray with Malathion, Dimethoate or Formothion every 10 days until clear.
SCALE INSECTS	Citrus, pineapple	Yellow to deep brown oval scales up to 6 mm (¼ in) long under leaves and on stems	Spray with Malathion every 10 days until all scales peel from leaf. Dimethoate also excellent.
SLUGS & SNAILS	Strawberries		Metaldehyde or Methiocarb pellets.
SLUGWORM	Pear, cherry	Black, slug-like caterpillars on upper surface of leaf	Spray with Fenitrothion, Malathion, or Derris.

PEST	ON CROPS	DESCRIPTION	ACTION
WHITEFLY	Melons under glass	Small white insects under leaves. Larvae minute	Permethrin at 10 day intervals until clear.

DISEASE	ON CROPS	DESCRIPTION	ACTION
GREY MOULD (BOTRYTIS)	Strawberry	Thick grey 'dust' on ripening fruit	Benomyl or Thiophanate-Methyl spray, every 10 days if necessary.
CANKER	Apples, some pears	Branches or trunk swollen. Bark dead and cracked	Cut out infected part, back to healthy wood. Check soil drainage (Canker worst in wet soils).
FIREBLIGHT	Pears	Shoots die, leaves look scorched and do not fall	Cut out and burn diseased wood to a point 60 cm (2 ft) beyond visibly infected tissue. Notify local branch of Ministry of Agriculture.
MILDEW, APPLE MILDEW, GOOSEBERRY MILDEW, POWDERY	Apple, quince, gooseberry, currant, peach, strawberries, grapes	All show first as white powdery particles on leaves and stems. May eventually form a complete coating, brownish on gooseberry fruits	Dinocap (if available), Benomyl, Thiophanate-Methyl sprays all good. If necessary, spray 2 or 3 times at 14 day intervals. Badly affected apple shoots can be pinched out and burnt.
PEACH LEAF CURL	Peaches, nectarines	Leaves curled and thickened, with reddish blisters	Collect and burn diseased leaves. Spray with copper based spray after leaf-fall, and as buds swell in Feb-March.
RUST	Plum	Yellow spots on upper surface of leaves. Only on weak trees	Burn affected leaves. Mulch and water tree next season.
SCAB	Apple, pear	Blackish or brownish patches on ripe fruit, hard and often splitting	Benomyl, Thiophanate-Methyl and Triforine all good. Spray at bud burst, and then fortnightly if trees badly affected previous season.
SILVER LEAF	Plums and allies, cherry, rarely apricots, currants and apples	Leaves at first silvered (*not* white), then brown and shrivelled. Shoots die	Cut out dead shoots or branches to 15 cm (6 in) behind infection. Paint wound with fungicidal paint. Wash pruning tools after use. Do not prune very susceptible crops in winter.

TOP FRUITS

ALMOND**

Prunus dulcis is a beautiful medium-sized tree, most often planted for its heavy sheaves of pure white or blush pink flowers. The crop is commercially important in many Mediterranean countries, where there are immense numbers of varieties. However, in good summers in favoured parts of England, some of them will yield large crops of excellent almonds.

The almond is closely related to the peach; the difference is that it has been selected to produce extralarge seeds (the almond is the kernel), and leathery flesh instead of the juicy flesh of the peach. The almond has similar leaves and suffers from the same diseases. To ensure regular crops, it should be grown against a wall like a peach. It is an interesting crop to grow, for fresh almonds have a unique flavour.

Even as far north as Fife, a wall crop will ripen every couple of years, whenever there is an Indian summer. Your supplier will be able to advise you about which varieties are self-fertile. 'Macrocarpa' produces excellent nuts.

Cultivation: Exactly the same as for peaches, except that some varieties will form short spurs on old wood. Encourage this by winter pruning side shoots of the main branches back to four buds or so.

Pests and diseases: Very much as for peaches (see page 44). Peach leaf curl can be a bit of a problem sometimes.

Harvesting: Leave the nuts on the tree as long as possible, but pick them by midautumn. Remove the green outer skin. The nuts can be eaten at once or stored in boxes of dry sand until you need them at Christmas.

APPLE*

This lovely and ancient fruit happily forms anything from a good sized tree to a single cordon. Whatever the shape, the trees are handsome in flower and when hung with ripe fruit; some even have perfumed blossoms. If you are prepared to be adventurous, and plant one of the very numerous lesser known varieties, some delicious things await you. 'Ashmead's Kernel' is a revelation.

As well as exhibiting variations in flavour, apple varieties ripen over a wide season. The earliest is available in late June, while the last to ripen is ready the following May. If you have a small garden, or one in which there are many other fruits, it is probably best to plant late-season types, even if you have to wrap and store them. It is more fun to munch your own apples in the depths of winter, than in summer when so many other fruits are very abundant.

Even if you only have room for cordons, plant as wide a range of apples as you can to give a number of different colours and tastes, rather than an enormous quantity of one sort. The other advantage of planting several varieties is that you will avoid pollination problems. Nevertheless, make sure that those you choose all belong to the same pollination group (see below). Do not be too concerned about achieving a balance between 'cooking' and 'dessert' types. While few cookers can be eaten raw, because they do not have enough sugar, most eaters can be cooked. They will not cook to the familiar purée-like texture, but for many recipes, especially older ones, this is an advantage.

Choosing varieties: Written descriptions of flavour and texture provide a basic guide. However, since different varieties do better in different parts of the country, the flavour varies too and it is best, if you can, to taste the ones that grow in your locality to find out what you like.

If you live in a cold part of the country, the latest maturing sorts of apple need to be grown against a wall, preferably south- or south-west facing.

If you are going to grow your plants in a heavily pruned form, avoid 'tip bearing' varieties like 'Bramley's Seedling' or 'Worcester Pearmain'. Though these will form spurs, young plants most often bear flower buds at the ends of last year's growths, so if they are heavily pruned, the flower buds will be cut away too. If you do want to grow them as

The seed, or kernel, of the almond is encased in the flesh

cordons or espaliers, leave part of last season's growth intact to ensure some flowers. In general, tip-bearers are best left to gardeners who can let them grow as bushes or half standards.

Most apple varieties prefer to be cross-pollinated; for some it is essential. For various complicated biological reasons, and because of different flowering times, the species is split into seven groups of varieties, all of which can pollinate other members of the same group. If you want to grow an unusual variety, check its pollination requirements with your supplier. Popular varieties of good flavour in the three biggest groups are:

Group 2

Egremont Russet	Oct-Dec
Ribston Pippin	Nov-Jan
St Edmund's Pippin	Sept-Oct
George Neal	Aug-Oct

Group 3

Cox's Orange Pippin	Oct-Dec
Discovery	Sept
Epicure	Aug-Sept
Katja	Sept-Oct
Kidd's Orange Red	Nov-Feb
Sunset	Nov-Dec
Worcester Pearmain	Sept-Oct
Blenheim Orange	Nov-Jan
Bramley's Seedling	Nov-Mar

Group 4

Ashmead's Kernel	Dec-Mar
Ellison's Orange	Sept-Oct
Orleans Reinette	Dec-Feb
Tydeman's Late Orange	Dec-Apr
Annie Elizabeth	Dec-Mar
Golden Noble	Sept-Jan
Lane's Prince Albert	Jan-Mar

Cultivation: The majority of apple varieties are remarkably easy to grow, being tolerant of a wide range of soils and climates. It is very easy to train apple trees into one of the artificial forms, and they can be used to make screens, low hedges, tunnels, arbours, and of course cordons and espaliers. For heavily pruned sorts, ensure that the trees are grafted on only a moderately dwarfing stock. For free standing bushes in a small garden, the stock should be the most dwarfing of all.

Spacing is important, for there's no point in wasting space, nor in trying to cram too many trees into too small an area. Single cordons are best planted 60 cm-1 m (2-3 ft) apart. Espaliers need a minimum of 4 m (12 ft), but will appreciate more if you have room. So that you don't waste valuable wall space while the espaliers are maturing, put redcurrants or gooseberries between the apples, and gradually grub them out as the espaliers expand. Bushes need at least 2 m (6 ft) spacings if on dwarfing stock. In a proper orchard, standard trees need planting at least 6.6 m (20 ft) apart. The ground beneath wall fruit can also be planted up. Bulbs are a good idea because they are below ground level when you need to spray the trees with tar oil.

The most important pruning takes place in winter, preferably in December or early January. This enables winter spraying to take place safely before the buds begin to expand.

For details of winter and summer pruning, see pages 16-17.

Pests and diseases: The more popular the fruits, the more prone they are to pests and diseases. Be vigilant. Even if you have a relatively problem-free garden, take care that no troubles begin to build up.

The most troublesome pests are codling moth and apple sawfly, while the most common diseases are canker and scab. For treatments, as well as prophylactics, see pages 28-29.

Harvesting and storage: Fallen apples and attentive birds will alert you to a ripening crop. Ripe apples will easily lift away from the branch.

Discovery apples flushed with colour and ready to harvest

Early ripening sorts need to be eaten at once, otherwise they turn soft and mealy. Harvest such varieties a little before they ripen, and keep them for a few days.

It is worth harvesting the entire crop of any variety that the birds are really partial to. They can ruin them all while looking for one ripe enough to eat. The level of attack seems to vary from year to year, so it is better to leave the fruit as long as you can. If it is harvested too long before ripening, it will not develop its full flavour.

Apples for winter should be left on the branch as long as possible, though not into the season of hard frosts. Pick them carefully, and place them with equal care into the basket or pail. Do not throw them in, or rot will set in

A small orchard of well-established apple trees in fruit

where the fruit has been bruised and will spread fast.

In the kitchen, wipe them over gently, wrap them in newspaper or proprietary fruit papers and pack them into boxes. It is also possible to keep the apples in polythene bags with breathing holes punched into them.

33

The apricot has beautiful
flowers, foliage and fruit

Allow about eight to ten apples to a bag, and place them loosely and in a single layer in boxes.

Apples must be stored somewhere cool and not too dry. A garage or well-shaded garden shed is excellent. If you have a modern house, do not use the loft to store apples: it is almost certainly too warm.

Over the subsequent weeks, check the fruit regularly for ripening. If more ripen than you can eat, remember that even wrinkled fruit cooks perfectly well.

APRICOT**

The apricot is a beautiful and vigorous tree, which when healthy covers itself with large white flowers in earliest spring, followed by bronzy pink young leaves. In late summer it produces luscious amber or yellowish fruits. The tree is perfectly hardy. Problems of cultivation are to do with its early flowering, vigour and the high temperatures needed to ripen the fruit. Except in the warmest parts of the warmest counties, the plants are best grown against a south-facing wall. Since even earlier flowering is the result, long before there are any bees about, hand pollination is necessary. As they are self-fertile this is not too difficult, and you only need one tree. If you do decide to grow an apricot, give it as much room as you can. Even on dwarfing stocks, they soon fill small spaces, and are then difficult to control. Do not try them on a wall less than 3 m (10 ft) high and

4.5 m (15 ft) across.

The most common variety is 'Moorpark', which generally fruits in August. It is named after a famous garden of the seventeenth century, when most wealthy squires grew apricots, and knew a good variety when they tasted one. Slightly earlier, and so more useful for northern gardeners, are the modern Canadian varieties 'Alfred' and 'Farmingdale'.

Cultivation: The fertilized flowers and young fruitlets may need some protection in harsh springs, or exposed situations. Draping the trees with netting is an effective protection from frost, but if necessary consider making up the sort of screens described on page 9. See what existing conditions can produce before undertaking this construction; I've seen an enormous and productive apricot enveloping part of a Scottish tower house, where no protection can have been offered.

Because the young branches are very pliable, apricots are easily trained into fans and espaliers, which is a very useful way of keeping the plant's vigour under the constant control it requires.

If you have sufficient space in the glasshouse, try growing in a pot an apricot that has been grafted on to a dwarfing stock, so that you do not have to wait long for fruit.

Pests and diseases: The apricot is a fairly tough crop. Various insects like the young leaves, however, and spraying may be necessary. As the fruit matures early, wasps can be a nuisance. If birds are a problem, use netting to keep them off.

Harvesting: If the fruit stays too long on the tree, the texture becomes mealy and much less pleasant to eat. Keep checking for sweetness once the fruit begins to soften. If you have had to thin out the clusters of fruits, try using the under-ripe ones in tarts and pies. Fully ripened ones are also excellent cooked in this way, as well as in jams and jellies.

CHERRY*

The cherry eventually grows into a large tree; since no dwarfing stock is yet available, they are not really suitable for small gardens. However, the trees give excellent value in the garden, since they are lovely not only in flower and fruit, but also in the autumn when the leaves take on dramatic colours. Because it is an exceptionally ancient species, there are many types and varieties, one or two of which may have been in cultivation since the Romans first brought the fruit to Europe.

Sweet cherries are derived from the bird cherry, and the gorgeous morello from the wild cherry. Duke cherries, which are worth growing if you can find them, are hybrids between these two. In small gardens the morello and duke types are much the most useful as they are self-fertile. Because they will also fruit nicely in shade, they can be grown against north-facing walls. As they are less vigorous than the sweet types, they can be trained as fans, but if you are happy with something less tidy, it is simplest to tie the soft whippy branches loosely to the wires. The less pruning done, the less chance there is of silver leaf infection setting in.

Sweet cherries can be trained as fans but only on the largest walls. You may do better to grow them as bushes in a fruit cage; eventually they will need heavy pruning, but you will have had several years of risk-free cropping by then. Cherries also grow quite nicely in pots. Providing the plants have had an abbreviated winter, they can be brought into warmth in January, and forced. By this means grand garden owners had cherries

Ripe cherries ready to be picked from a well-trained tree

all year round, something few gardeners now manage. If growing sweet cherries, you'll need two varieties and a paint brush. Try 'Early Rivers' with 'Bigarreau de Schrecken' or 'Merton Heart'; 'Merton Bigarreau' with 'Kent Bigarreau' or 'Napoleon Bigarreau'. 'Bigarreau' indicates that the cherry has slightly crisp flesh. There are other delicious cherries to be had, many of which will happily accept pollen from the morello.

Cultivation: Cherries do well on a variety of soils, as long as they are well fed. Apply an annual mulch of rotted manure or compost. Add wood ash, or a light dressing of a potash-rich fertilizer.

If planting free-standing trees, bear in mind the difficulty of protecting the ripening fruit from birds. You are bound to lose the fruit on the upper branches, but it is possible to enclose the lower ones in large tubes of netting and thus manage to keep some of your crop. Otherwise, it might be worth trying some of the model hawks available. Commercial orchardists use a gas gun; you must not.

If you want to try cherries against a wall, sweet sorts like south, west or east aspects. Sweet cherries, too, can be made to spur fairly easily; once the basic structure has been built up, prune lateral shoots in summer to six leaves; prune again in early autumn to three buds. Do not prune in winter.

Sour cherries (including the dukes) do not short-spur. The best way to treat them is to cut out a certain amount of fruited wood each year, and so encourage the production of new wood, while still keeping the tree within the bounds of the wall. Cherries can be grown as bushes in the fruit cage using the same methods.

Pests and diseases: Keep a constant check for aphis, the worst insect pest, and slugworm. Silver leaf disease can be a problem if you have made the mistake of doing some winter pruning. Bullfinches can take the flower buds, and other species will completely clear the trees of ripe fruit, or – which is more frustrating – damage every one while looking for the ripest. Wall fruit is most easily protected, but take care to do it thoroughly. Birds find cherries devastatingly attractive and will find the tiniest chink that will let them into the fruit.

Harvesting: Once the colour has developed to its maximum, keep tasting for the sort of sweetness you like. The stalks of sweet cherries come away from the branch very easily. Sour cherries require more care; pulling too hard can remove leaves, stem and all. Use small sharp scissors to cut the stalks. When harvested, eat the cherries at once; alternatively they may be bottled, soaked in brandy, or made into an excellent cherry wine.

CRAB APPLE*

Many of the decorative forms of crab apple are to be seen, their showy flowers and colourful leaves vying for vividness with the ripe fruits. The

The fruits of the crab apple are produced in large clusters

culinary crab apples flower prodigiously too, have a rather stronger perfume than most true apples (a tree can, on a good day, waft scent over the whole garden), and produce large quantities of clustered fruit in yellow, amber and scarlet.

If you want a productive tree for the front garden, where true apples would never get a chance to ripen, try planting a crab. You will be surprised how useful the fruit is. A small quantity added to an apple pie vastly improves the flavour, and even the best apple jelly seems insipid once you have

tried making it with a good proportion of crabs. Pure crab apple jelly is exquisite. Apple wine, too, is all the better made with the addition of a few crab apples.

The variety usually suggested for culinary use is 'John Downie', with nice oblong apples of golden yellow flushed with rose on one side. It looks splendid while the fruit is ripening and before the birds realize they are missing something good. The taste is excellent. There are other good varieties, however, so try them if you can. 'Golden Hornet' and 'Red Sentinel' are both splendid.

Cultivation: Grow crab apples very much as you would apples. There is no advantage in enriching the soil except when the tree is first planted, nor in growing crabs against a wall. No pruning is needed except to keep the tree reasonably open and healthy.

Pests and diseases: Some varieties are susceptible to scab. Spray as for apples. The varieties suggested above are immune.

Harvesting: Leave the fruit as late as you can, and certainly well into September. Thereafter, the birds will begin to reduce the crop. The little apples will keep well in a cool place for a week or two if you cannot use them at once.

DAMSON**

A member of the vast plum tribe, the damson borrows many characteristics from the wild bullace. The result is a smallish tree, usually less than 9 m (30 ft) high, often narrow leafed, and exceptionally hardy and storm resistant. Although the flowers are small and without much substance, they appear early enough in the year to compensate for their insignificance. The fruits are small, blackish purple outside, amber yellow within. The flesh is disappointing eaten raw, but a delectable and unique taste develops as soon as it is cooked.

The trees are happy in most soils and in the least sheltered of situations, but they prefer the eastern counties of Britain with cold win-

ters and, it is to be hoped, hot dry summers. Damsons produce prodigious crops when well suited to the growing conditions.

Some varieties are self-fertile; others cross easily with either damsons or true plums. Try using damsons as windbreaks for choice dessert plums. They are easily trained against west- or east-facing walls, either as fans or espaliers, though plums or greengages better deserve the space. On a wall, damsons

The damson will crop well in favourable conditions

may need hand pollinating.

'Farleigh Damson' has fruit of excellent flavour, but needs pollinating by another variety. Use 'Oulin's Gage' or even the plum 'Kirke's'. 'Merryweather' will self-pollinate, but its flavour is somewhat inferior.

Cultivation: Damsons can be grown in unpromising conditions, but they will benefit from good soil, fed with nit-

rogen and potash. Otherwise, treat as plums (see page 48).

Pests and diseases: As for plums. Aphis like damson foliage, so keep checking for them and for various caterpillars. Investigate all curled leaves. Winter sprays of tar oil are helpful preventives.

Harvesting: Pick the fruit when it softens. As damsons are less sweet than most plums, birds and wasps are less of a problem. Picked fruit will store in a cool place for a week or two.

ELDER*

Now often regarded as a hedgerow weed and garden nuisance, the elder was once of enormous domestic importance, furnishing salads and pickles, insecticides, medicines, flavourings, jellies, wine and jam.

Nowadays, it is still used for flavouring – elderflowers make gooseberry jam divine – and for wine and jelly. If you want to grow an elder rather than raid the flowers and fruit of the countryside, there is no reason to have the rank-looking wild form in your garden. Many decorative forms are available, some of which are outstanding.

A form that was popular with the Elizabethans is the cut-leafed elder, the leaflets of which are deeply cut and jagged, almost like some of the Japanese maples; the mature plants have considerable grace. There are also elders with variegated leaves, and a particularly fine form with golden leaves and scarlet berries. The flowers and fruit of all are quite as good as those of the wild elder, and all are quite easily propagated from cuttings of young wood.

Cultivation: Elders will do happily in most soils and in most situations. They flower and fruit best in full sun, but will still give a useful crop in shade.

Pests and diseases: None.

Harvesting: Pick the flowers whenever most of those on a particular bunch are open. If they are to be used as a flavouring in jams or custards, put the flowers in a muslin bag to avoid leaving a trail of petals in whatever you are cooking.

Like grapes, the fruit darkens some while before the berries are fully ripe. Keep checking for taste, or watch to see if the birds are beginning

to enjoy themselves.

FIG*

The fig is a marvellous plant with bold foliage and a picturesque shape; its exquisite fruit – green, purple or brown skinned – has flesh in various shades of dusky pink.

In warm parts of the country, a good single crop of figs can be had from free-standing plants. Elsewhere, the trees need the protection of a south-facing wall. For these there is always plenty of competition, but a dish of properly ripened figs, sweet and perfumed, is a strong inducement to give a fig some space.

Under glass, even without much heat, most varieties of fig can be persuaded to give

two crops, the first developing from young fruit buds that have withstood the winter, the second from fruit buds on the earliest part of the new growth. A much wider range of sorts can be grown as well, many with flavours far superior to the commoner kinds.

Outdoors, most figs, which are native to hot, dry Mediterranean countries, adapt to our climate by producing masses of foliage and few mature fruits. Most need to be planted in situations where there is a very restricted root run. Sunken brick boxes containing about

The luscious ripening fruit of 'Brown Turkey' fig

1 m³ (35 ft³) of soil are the usual arrangements. The box has no bottom, but the lowest 22-30 cm (9-12 inches) is filled with coarse rubble or gravel which will prevent the roots from exploring outside.

Figs also fruit well in large pots or tubs, though they need to stand somewhere sheltered. Large plants are easily toppled by a sudden summer gale.

The most frequently seen variety is 'Brown Turkey', unusual in that it does not need to have its roots cramped and can be planted in open ground. The fruit is not large or in the first rank for flavour. 'White Marseilles' is delicious and reliable, if you restrict its roots. It does well in pots.

Cultivation: Against a wall, or under glass, figs are best trained as fans. When the fan is full-grown, some of the major spokes need to be removed every few years to ensure new growth, and so fruit, at the centre. Alternatively, cuttings will root very easily, so overgrown and unproductive trees are quite easily replaced.

Do not leave figs grown outdoors to fend for themselves in winter. New wood may be killed by the cold, and you will lose the chance of fruit in the following summer. Provide some protection; the usual method with a fan is to untie the spokes, bunch them together, and cover them in a straw coat. If you have not pruned the fig, this will not be possible.

Under glass, it is tempting to leave the half-matured fruit to over-winter in the hope that they will ripen next year.

Some will, but the rest will begin to rot when spring comes, and the rot will spread down the stalk and into the branch itself. Remove the fruits in autumn to protect the tiny buds higher up.

Pests and diseases: Under glass, red spider can be a nuisance. Hose the leaves every few days. The ripening fruit is attractive to woodlice, who start eating at the junction of stalk and fruit.

Outdoors, birds are the main problem. Put nets over the plants when the fruit is ripening. This is easier than bagging each fig individually, though this keeps wasps away too. Figs ripen in sequence, so if you do use bags, each one can be used to protect several figs.

Harvesting: When the fruit ripens, the skin near the fruit's opening begins to split, revealing the juicy flesh. By that stage, the fig should come away from the branch easily.

Some people are slightly allergic to the skin of the fig. It is perfectly easy to remove this, starting at the split.

FILBERT*

An ancient and very underused crop, filberts are related to cob and hazelnuts (see below). They are easy to grow and are very flexible, providing low bushes or medium-sized trees. They look attractive hung with catkins in earliest spring, grow well in shade, and provide a prodigal and delicious crop.

Cultivation: The yield may be disappointing if but a single variety is planted. This is because the tiny and bril-

liantly coloured styles are not always receptive when the catkins are shedding pollen. The answer is to plant several sorts, so that the styles of one will take the pollen of another variety.

Except in large gardens where plants can be left to grow as they please, it is best to grow filberts as bushes at 3.6 m (12 ft) spacings. If used to edge a path, especially a grass one with a border of primulas and spring bulbs, filberts are easily pruned into

hedges to make a pleasant spring and summer walk. Alternatively, the plants can be allowed to grow high enough to arch overhead and cast a delicate shade.

In small gardens, the plants can be tied to wires stretched between posts, perhaps as a productive screen to the kitchen garden. If you have an unused north facing wall and do not want to clothe it with a morello cherry, then a filbert can be planted to make a productive espalier.

Filberts, which are narrow nuts with thin shells, not fully covered by the green husk, and cobnuts, which are round, thick shelled nuts, entirely covered by the husk, taste very much the same, though 'Purple Filbert' and 'Red Filbert' are sometimes suggested as the best. The red catkins and dramatic purple leaves of the purple type make it a decorative addition to the garden. 'Lambert's Filbert' is an ancient variety with succulent and delicious

Purple-leaved varieties of filbert are very decorative

kernels. 'Pearson's Prolific' is useful if you want a naturally low-growing form.

Pests and diseases: Few organisms attack the crop, at least until the nuts start ripening. Thereafter, squirrels and mice can be problems calling for drastic remedies.

Harvesting: The nuts are ready to be picked when they begin to separate easily from the husk. Keep checking, or gales will disperse the crop, especially filberts, which slip from their husks. Harvest the nuts still with their frilled covering. They look much prettier served like that, and the husk also serves to stop the nuts drying out too much before you want to eat them.

When harvested, the nutshells will still be fairly green. Leave them in a cool place until the shells have fully darkened. The nuts should still remain in reasonable condition until well into the new year.

GREENGAGE**

The name greengage was originally given to a remarkable and ancient variety of plum with a delicious aroma and sweet green flesh. However, as members of the group hybridise easily, there are now several sorts of gage, as well as true plums with a gage flavour.

The greengage is native to Turkey but had reached France by the sixteenth century where it is still known as *Reine Claude*, named after the queen who is supposed to have imported it. It probably reached Britain soon after. It was reintroduced in the eighteenth century, from which time the name 'greengage' dates.

The varieties of gage which are now available have either green or yellow skins which are often rather thick. The trees will flourish over much of the country, but only in the warmest regions will they do as orchard trees. A south- or west-facing wall is necessary elsewhere.

'Denniston's Superb' is the hardiest and best cropper, having also the advantage of self-fertility. 'Early Transparent' is the most delicious, and trains well as a fan. The original greengage can still be found, though it is not a reliable cropper. Also grown is 'Reine Claude de Bavay', a variant of the ancient sort which took its name from the French queen. It is a late cropper and easy to grow, but the fruit has only a moderate flavour.

Cultivation: Treat greengages as plums, but give them better soil and a warm position.

Pests and diseases: As for plums. Woolly aphis seem to like greengages. Look for them underneath the leaves if you see wasps showing an unseasonal interest in the area. Use nets against wasps and birds homing in early on the crop, or tie plastic 'flappers' to the branches. The fruit stalks are too short to be able to use bags.

Harvesting: The fruit is ready for picking when it is subtly yellowed – or even translucent – and aromatic. You will probably have to harvest before this point is reached, however, to avoid the worst damage the birds and wasps can inflict. On a windowsill or pantry shelf, the fruit will ripen satisfactorily, and the flavour will still be very good, though not absolute perfection. A very good way of preparing under-ripe greengages for the table is to poach them in wine and vanilla-flavoured sugar.

MEDLAR*

An extremely pretty and very hardy medium-sized tree, the medlar becomes picturesque with age. Flowering from the end of May, the tree sports substantial cream, later pinkish, flowers at the tip of each branchlet. The oval leaves soon darken becoming in autumn a spectacular mixture of tan, bronze and purple. The tree makes a splendid 'specimen' for the focal point of a lawn.

The fruit, differing slightly in shape from one variety to another, looks like a small brown pear, with very long sepals left over from the vanished flower. They remain hard well into autumn, and are proof against birds and children. The fruit should be harvested sometime in October – a pleasant task for a sunny weekend – before they fall from the tree. Store them in a pantry or other cool place until the fruit softens (or becomes 'bletted') some time in November and December.

The flavour and texture are slightly odd, and are perhaps something of an acquired taste. The flavour is reminiscent of both over-ripe apples and rosehips. Medlar jelly is delicious.

If you would like large fruits on a decorative tree of weeping habit, choose the variety called 'Dutch'. If you want smaller fruits on an upright, and more manageable tree, plant 'Nottingham'.

Cultivation: Medlars are not fussy about soil, but like plenty of light and, if possible, some shelter. The young leaves are easily damaged by strong winds. Feed the trees in their first year or two to

The curiously shaped medlar fruits remain hard until after they are harvested

encourage strong early growth. Thereafter, they need little attention.

Medlars are usually grafted on to hawthorn stocks. These are very flexible on young plants, so make sure that the tree has a good strong stake.

Pests and diseases: are few.
Harvesting: See above.

MULBERRY*

It is difficult to know why the mulberry is now so rarely grown. It is a most beautiful tree in its own right, easy and fast to grow, and makes a splendid and picturesque 'specimen'. It is also easy to train as a fan or espalier, and crops bountifully when so treated. The fruit ripens from pink to deepest ruby, and is so full of juice that it is impossible to eat without stained fingers. The flavour is sharp and sweet at the same time, and deliciously fragrant. A dish of mulberries gives a grand finish to a late summer meal. They make a full-flavoured jelly and a good wine.

Make sure you plant only the black mulberry, *Morus nigra*. The white sort has fruits which are oddly bland, and not worth eating, though silkworms adore the leaves.

The only disadvantage of the mulberry is that young trees can take eight to ten years to fruit, so they are something of a long-term investment. By that time, they are also very attractive to look at. Try planting one or two as soon as you move to a new garden.

Cultivation: Plant in spring if possible. Mulberries are happy in most soils. They do well in the lawn, and even better against walls, whether pruned or not. Since they are obedient to train, form an espalier to make the best use of wall space. Mature trees sometimes need support for the lower boughs, but this only adds charm to their venerable appearance. They're particularly good if you want to grow strawberries beneath (or bulbs, if you want flowers). Since the trees are the last of all garden plants to come into leaf, this gives strawberry or bulb foliage plenty of time, and light, to mature.

Pests and diseases: Starlings and thrushes take the fruits while they are still firm and on the tree. Blackbirds take them once they have fallen. Mature trees fruit so abundantly that if you can scare only that species away, you will do reasonably well.

Harvesting: When the fruit is ripe, it falls naturally to the ground, so the best specimens are always gathered from beneath the tree. Provide something to soften their landing, even a plastic sheet, so that they do not bruise. Both this, and basic protection, are easiest for wall grown plants. If protection and harvesting are a problem, pick the fruit while firm, and use it for jelly or jam. If it is undamaged, spread it out on shelves to ripen a little more.

NECTARINE**/***

Nectar indeed is this wonderful variant of the peach. The genetic difference is so slight that very occasionally branches of peach trees are said to bear nectarines. This is quite a transformation, for the skins of nectarines are shiny, without down, and the flesh is firm. This does not stop them from being lusciously juicy, with a sumptuous flavour. If you want to make the most of a small sunny wall, or a small greenhouse, nectarines are the trees to grow. They may be a little less hardy than peaches, but still do well outdoors in parts of Scotland.

Two nectarine varieties are to be recommended 'Early Rivers', which is easily obtainable and delicious, and 'Lord Napier' of even better flavour but not so commonly found.

Cultivation and pests and diseases: are as you might expect, the same as for the peach.

Harvesting: Nectarines remain on the tree as they ripen. As the colour deepens and the perfume gets stronger, keep checking them with a gentle touch to see if the flesh is softening. It is not as soft as that of the peach. You will probably find that as you test the flesh the fruits detach themselves from the tree.

PEACH**/***

It is difficult to know why so few people grow their own peaches. In most of the southern counties, peaches crop heavily as free-standing trees, and they are fairly easy to manage against a wall, in a pot or under glass. At one time most farmhouses, and every manor, grew peaches in many varieties and in substantial quantities. Some sorts, like 'Peregrine', have showy flowers before they fruit. Whatever the flower, a ripe peach eaten straight from the tree on a summer morning is one of the greatest pleasures of the season.

Cultivation: Peaches thrive in any well-drained soil. In general, it is best not to feed them too heavily, or the foliage becomes too luxuriant, making pruning and training harder, and keeping sunlight from the fruit.

On walls, they are usually treated as fans, using the 'long spur' system (see pages 16–17). Under glass, either grow them as bushes in large pots, using high-yielding varieties on dwarfing rootstock, or plant them out in cold greenhouse borders.

Peaches were traditionally grown in south-facing lean-to greenhouses, with the trees trained up the back wall. In modern free-standing greenhouses, it is possible to train the trees up the inside of the glass, attaching the branches

o wire stretched along the main struts of the greenhouse. The main disadvantage is that the spurs and their replacements grow upwards and touch the glass. As a result, the leaves are scorched by hot sun.

If the greenhouse is large enough, it is simplest to plant the trees in the centre. The main pruning, to keep them within bounds and allow you room to move, takes place in winter.

Many people seem to think that peaches need winter heat, but they do not. Heat is only necessary in earliest spring if you want to force an early crop and that is only useful if you want to sell the produce. Peaches grown in unheated greenhouses bear fruit just as the price of imported peaches begins to

A crop of good-sized nectarines ripening under glass

drop. Whatever the price, it is still a treat to have your own. Even a small tree will yield plenty of fruit.

Under glass, the flowers need hand-pollination. The trees are self-fertile. For tall plants in which the uppermost flowers are difficult to reach, try attaching the

45

Even quite a small peach tree will yield a rewarding crop

handle of the paintbrush to the end of a bamboo cane.

Do not let plants dry out in the early stages of fruit formation otherwise the fruits open at the base and begin to rot. It is particularly important to keep potted specimens well watered.

Prune young side shoots which are not needed to extend the tree or for replacement 'spurs' to four leaves when this can easily be done. It is essential to thin out young fruitlets. It is tempting not to do this, especially when the tree is young, and the gardener greedy for plenty of fruit; but the tree will only reward your negligence with small fruits of poor flavour, if any.

Peach varieties are avail-able with different periods of ripening, flesh and skin colour and flavour. In general, the white-fleshed sorts have the best flavour. 'Peregrine' is a good one, and often seen. 'Rochester', later-ripening, is red-skinned but not of quite as good flavour.

If you have a big tree or two, you will soon have plenty of self-sown seedlings. Do not bother with them: peaches do not come true from seed, and though there is a very slim chance you might discover some ravishing variety, seedlings take many years to fruit and most will waste your time.

Pests and diseases: The main scourge of outdoor peaches is peach leaf curl disease (see page 29). Birds, of course, attack the ripening fruit. Net the trees, or put individual peaches in bags.

Under glass, red spider is a constant threat which, if not controlled, will destroy the tree. Spray with insecticide, or simply hose down with water every other day or so. It is possible to introduce a predator insect that will eat up the red spiders, but this is expensive and does not always work. It is not advisable to grow grapes and peaches in the same house; grapes need to be dry, so spiders attack the peach leaves ravenously. Woodlice can be a problem where the fruit joins the stalk. Keep an eye out for them.

Harvesting: Although it is always a pleasure, peaches are best picked in the morning. If anything more than the lightest tug is needed leave the fruit on the branch It is not ripe. Better still, let the peach fall off. Rig up netting beneath the tree to stop the fruit bruising itself on the ground or, under glass, pile crumpled newspaper beneath the branches. The fruit is sometimes damaged in falling, but the odd dent doesn't interfere with the perfect flavour.

Peaches only last at their peak for a few hours, or a day at the most. They can be kept in the refrigerator for a day or two, but are then best used for cooking.

PEAR*/**

The owner of two good pear trees, or more, enjoys something of a privilege. Pears on their own roots, or grafted on to pear seedlings, make large and handsome trees, thick with flowers in spring, and hung in summer with huge quantities of fruit which last until you rush out to save them from local starlings. Nowadays, pears are commonly found grafted on to one of the quince stocks. This keeps them to a smaller size, but makes them rather trickier to grow.

The fruit itself can also be tricky to manage. Unlike apples, pears remain in eatable condition for a very short time. Some gourmets claim that perfection lasts but an hour or two. Unripe pears are too hard to eat, though they may be poached, preferably in red wine, but over-ripe ones are only fit for the compost heap. However, a good pear, in its short prime, is one of the most glorious fruits, being really juicy, sweet, and richly fragrant.

That there is a large number of varieties with a corresponding range of flavours is not surprising in such an ancient and important crop. Good ones are listed below in their pollination groups.

Cultivation: Pears on pear stocks will grow on a wide range of soils, even on those that would support no other fruit. On quince stocks, they need good rich garden soil, with plenty of moisture and rich in nitrogen. Such trees need feeding every year with a good mulch of manure or compost.

Since pears are quite as tractable as apples, they can be trained and pruned in exactly the same way. Ensure that wall fruits never lack moisture, for the ground at the base of old walls can be very free draining.

Conference pears are self-fertile and will produce fruit from a single tree

Some pears suffer from wind damage so check before planting, and provide some wind cover if possible. 'Conference' is the most vulnerable in this respect.

Because many dessert pears ripen late in the season, gardeners in cold counties should plant slightly less choice, early-maturing sorts. Do not despise old varieties with small fruits. 'Jargonelle' is ancient, but the fruits are delicious, and it does well in cold, even shady, conditions. Remember, too, that the cooking pears make excellent winter eating, baked or stewed, and go a lovely rosy colour in the cooking.

Pollination needs to be considered. Some varieties are fairly self-fertile, and so a single tree can be planted. 'Conference' is the usual one suggested, but there are others. Check with your supplier. In general, it is much better to plant two trees of different varieties. As with apples, the crop is split into several pollination groups. While it can be very rewarding to find and grow some of the unusual sorts, delicious and widely available varieties are listed here in pollination groups:

Group 2

Louise Bonne of Jersey	Oct-Nov
Packham's Triumph	Nov

Group 3

Beurré Hardy	Oct
Beurré Superfin	Oct
Conference	Oct
*Jargonelle	Aug
Joséphine de Malines	Dec-Jan

*William's Bon Chrétien	Sept

* = suitable for a north wall

Group 4

Doyenné de Comice	Nov
Onward	Sept-Oct
Catillac (cooking)	until Apr
Pitmaston Duchess (cooking)	Oct until Feb

Although pears produce flowers in substantial bunches, it is best not to let them fruit in the same manner. Where possible, thin each cluster to one or two fruits. If you do not thin them out you will have large quantities of small fruits. Unlike peaches and nectarines, however, the flavour will not be too much impaired.

Pests and diseases: The worst disease is scab (see page 29), which can be devastating on some varieties. Others, like 'Catillac', 'Hessle' and 'Dr Jules Guyot' are never infected.

Peach midge can be a nuisance in some gardens. Have a close look if some fruitlets are distorted and discoloured; there may be tiny maggots inside. If there are, there is little you can do until next season, except burn all infected fruits. Next year, spray with BHC at early white bud stage.

Birds are the worst pest. Starlings, tits and blackbirds are attracted by the ripening fruit. A flock of starlings can ruin an entire crop in an afternoon, not only by eating ripe fruits, but stabbing all the others to see if they're ready. Where feasible, put up nets or bird scarers, or bag individual fruits.

Harvesting: How and when

A heavy crop of Comice pears illustrates the importance of thinning the clusters of fruit

pears ripen depends on variety, locality, season and location in the garden, so experience is the surest guide. In general, pick fruit just before final ripening. At this stage, the pear should lift easily from the tree. Handle the fruit carefully, for although the flesh will still be hard, bruises now will cause uneven ripening.

Store the picked fruit somewhere cool, keeping ones you want to eat soon somewhere warmer. Later-ripening varieties will take anything up to several months to soften and become ripe. Since they need frequent checking it is unwise to wrap and box them. In any case they do not usually shrivel in the way that unwrapped apples do. Test them both by smell, and by gently pressing the fruit. You will soon become good at detecting fruit at the peak for eating. Unless you have somewhere cool to store the fruit, you may find that an entire crop has ripened more or less simultaneously. This is one reason why, if you have several varieties, they should be chosen with a spread of ripening times.

Cooking pears never soften. Most varieties can be used throughout the winter.

PLUMS*/**

From July to the end of September, plums of yellow, amber, ruby and deepest purple can grace the table. Use them fresh or stew them

with red wine and vanilla sugar to make sumptuous desserts. Delicious bottled plums will last you through the winter. All plum varieties make marvellous jams.

Plums of most sorts are fairly easy to grow in all but the coldest wettest parts of the country, and do exceptionally well against walls if you can give them one of sufficient height. They are attractive when in flower, and look magnificent when the branches are loaded, sometimes to breaking point, with translucent fruit.

If you are prepared to plant something other than the reliable 'Victoria', there are some delicious alternatives. One of the reasons why so many people plant 'Victoria'

is that because it is self-fertile, only one tree is needed. There are other self-fertile varieties worth considering, particularly 'Czar' and 'Warwickshire Drooper'. The most delicious of the dessert plums, 'Kirke's', is self-sterile, and needs something to fertilize it. You should also try 'Count Althann's Gage'.

The plum family includes greengages and damsons, which are described on pages 42 and 37, and bullaces and myrobalans. The latter pair make pretty garden trees, and are especially useful where pests create problems. The crops from each can be heavy, and both make excellent jams and jellies.

Cultivation: Plums are happy in most locations. Areas subject to late frosts are not suit-able, however, as flower and fruitlets can be damaged. Wall fruits are usually safe from frosts. Indeed, in the North of England and in Scotland the choicer varieties must have the shelter of a wall. If they are grafted on the dwarfing stock St Julien A, plums can fairly easily be trained as fans, and some of the less vigorous types, even as espaliers. 'Victoria' does nicely in this form. Check the vigour of stock and scion with your supplier. Allow at least 4.5 m (15 ft) of wall for a fan, and as much between plants if you are putting in dwarf bushes. It is preferable to buy maiden plants and do the initial pruning yourself. Remember to prune only between June and August, otherwise your plants may

The rich-coloured 'Czar' plum is a self-fertile cooking variety

contract silver leaf disease.

Plums need to have plenty of nourishment, especially when young. Mulch annually with compost or else with rotted manure.

In cold springs, fruits against a south wall may flower before the bees are around. Use a paintbrush to assist pollination. If you have planted varieties that need crossing, pick a bunch of flowers from one plant and brush it against the flowers of the other (and vice versa).

Plums may crop very heavily. The fruits can be thinned, which will give you a smaller number of larger fruits. It may be necessary to ensure that the branches do not break when fully laden by tying them to canes or poles as supports.

Pests and diseases: See the chart on page 28. Aphis are the commonest pest. Keep a lookout for them, especially underneath young leaves. If you see wasps visiting a tree long before the fruit is ripe, check for woolly aphis. The wasps themselves later cause damage to the fruit, but there is little you can do about them. Greedy birds can be put off by flying a row of plastic strips near each tree (see page 26).

Harvesting: The activities of the largest pests will alert you to the ripening fruit. Plums may soften rather before they are sweet enough to eat. If you cannot keep the pests away, harvest the fruits as they soften, and store them on a shelf in the kitchen, pantry or garage. You will lose a little of the flavour as the fruit subsequently ripens, which may take several days, or even a week or two, but there will be plenty to eat. After ripening, the fruit will last on the shelf for about a fortnight or so.

If you cannot wait for the fruit to ripen, bake it. The aroma is truly exquisite.

QUINCE*

This lovely plant is usually in the form of a large bush with drooping branches, but some varieties make a medium-sized tree, densely leafed, and of picturesque appearance. It should not be confused with the Japanese quince, *Chaenomeles japonica*, which is much smaller, has more colourful flowers and vastly inferior fruit. The true quince is *Cydonia oblonga*. Its flowers appear once the first flush of leaves have matured in late May or early June, and they sit above the leaves like small pale pink waterlilies.

Trees look magnificent in autumn, hung with large greeny-gold and mottled fruits which, after harvesting, leave deep yellow foliage behind. In the Near and Middle East, where quinces have been grown for many thousands of years, they ripen sufficiently to be eaten directly from the tree. Here, they almost never soften, and need to be cooked in pies, or turned into beautifully coloured jellies and jams. The

The true quince, Cydonia oblonga, produces delicious-looking fruit for cooking

Latin for quince is *marmelo*, and is the origin of marmalade.

Only a few varieties are now available of the dozens of variously shaped quinces that once existed. 'Portugal' is good, oval, and deepens almost to orange if kept ripening. The tree is vigorous, but sometimes flowers too early to crop well. 'Meech's Prolific' has pear-shaped fruit, and lives up to its name. 'Vranja' or 'Champion' are also recommended.

Cultivation: Quinces like damp soil, and do well in a certain amount of shade. They are not fussy about soil, but the large and rather soft leaves need some shelter. All varieties do very well against a wall, and the pliable young growth is easily tied on to wires.

It is worth feeding young plants with a mulch of well-rotted compost, but older ones can look after themselves. Pruning is simply a matter of keeping the tree reasonably open, and keeping the more inconvenient branches under control.

Pests and diseases: Quinces are remarkably trouble-free. Leaves that become red, then black, have quince leaf blight. Cut out diseased shoots, and next season spray with a copper fungicide as the first leaves unfurl in spring. Apple mildew is a rare visitant. Birds occasionally nip out the petals of young flowers.

Harvesting: Do not pick the fruits until they have at least begun to yellow, and the perfume reached full strength. Take them indoors before the first frosts. Store on open shelves in the pantry, or wrap like apples and store in a box. Keep them away from apples and pears, as these will pick up the quinces' distinctive aroma.

When cooking, only use the flesh. Discard the seeds and their packing, or the flavour will be bitter.

VINE***

This delectable crop is not at all difficult to grow, but requires fairly constant work from mid-spring to autumn to ensure a good crop. Even a small vine can supply a large quantity of fruit.

In favoured parts of the southern counties, vines can be grown as free-standing plants in vineyards, but most dessert grapes do best against a south-facing wall. In such a situation grapes will fruit well quite far north and even the warmer parts of Scotland can produce good fruit in an exceptional season.

Many amateurs will achieve the best results in a greenhouse or conservatory, whether there is room for one large pot, yielding perhaps a dozen good bunches, or for a full-sized vine yielding hundreds. A slightly heated greenhouse would permit some of the choicer late-ripening grapes to be grown, particularly the various muscats, whose fine flavour amply repays the cost of heating in spring and autumn.

The choice of varieties now available is increasing, reflecting a renewed interest in the vine. Many are most suited to the wine producer, but good dessert varieties include 'Siegerrebe', and the various 'Chasselas' and 'Strawberry' types for walls outdoors; 'Black Hamburgh', 'Forster's Seedling' and 'Buckland Sweetwater' are for cold greenhouses, 'Frontignan' is good for pots, and the marvellous 'Muscat of Alexandria' for slightly heated greenhouses.

Vines are ornamental in their own right. The leaves are handsome, the plants graceful, and the clusters of berries spectacular. For even more visual effect, choose from the varieties with particularly decorative leaves. The one called either 'Incana' or 'Dusty Miller' has leaves heavily dusted with white meal; 'Purpurea' has deep purplish foliage which looks handsome when grown near

Training a newly planted vine

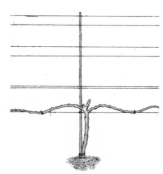 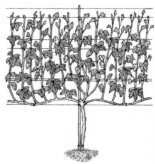

some of the more refined and pale-coloured clematis, and the leaves of 'Brandt' go a magnificent scarlet in autumn to set off the berries.

Cultivation: Vines are vigorous plants which must be pruned frequently and ruthlessly if a picturesque but barren tangle is not to be the result.

Vines grown in pots can be treated in the same way as raspberries, with two canes allowed, one from last year to fruit, one of this year to grow. The old cane will attempt to grow too, but stop it by pinching out the main growing tip and all the side shoots four to six leaves after the flower truss if there is one, two if not. Allow only one shoot, the lowest, to grow and make a new cane. In deepest winter, cut the fruited shoot back to two buds (easily visible), above the junction with next year's fruit cane. If both buds want to grow next spring, rub out the topmost one.

Grown against a wall, or in the greenhouse, a simple way to train a plant is to cut back the newly planted vine to three to four buds if you have glass to ground level, higher if not. Let two shoots develop, and train them horizontally along wires to right and left. Next year, allow buds to develop every 30 cm (12 inches) and train them vertically. You should now have a fork-shaped plant, with as many tines as you have room for. Thereafter treat each cane as you would a potted plant.

It is possible to grow vines as espaliers although difficul-

Thin out the leaves around a bunch of grapes to let in light

ties arise when the available space is filled, and it is said that grapes from new wood taste better than those from old. Certainly, the bunches are often smaller.

Take great care not to let vast amounts of foliage develop. Ripening grapes need sun and warmth for flavour, and the free movement of air is important, as the bunches

of fruits are less likely to rot. Thin the leaves out if they become too dense and use them in the kitchen, whether for dolmathes, wrapping chickens for roasting, or baked with mushrooms and a little garlic.

The flowers will be opening by early June. Outdoors, pollination is no problem. Indoors, the clusters need tapping gently with a cane to shake pollen on to the stigmas. You should be able to

53

see the falling dust. If you get a shower of tiny green petals, you're too late. Vine flowers have a wonderful, though very subtle fragrance.

When the young fruitlets begin to form, the bunches must be thinned out by about half to leave the remainder room to develop. Equip yourself with a pair of scissors with long narrow blades. Surgical scissors are suitable in the absence of proper vine scissors. Snip away at each bunch, trying to clear the fruitlets away from the centre. In general, you can cut out whole bunchlets. Pay special attention to the top or 'shoulder' of each bunch.

Continue nipping out unwanted vegetative growth and when the berries are one third their full size, have another look over each bunch. Once again, they will be congested. Using a twig, small spatula or an eraser-tipped pencil, lift up each

Young grape fruitlets must be thinned out hard

branch of the bunch and snip out yet more fruit. Experience will tell you how much to cut out, but once more about half the fruitlets should go. The aim is to get a well-filled bunch, but one in which each berry has room to swell, and in which air can freely circulate. Without this drastic thinning, the berries will be impossibly cramped, will burst, and the whole bunch suddenly rot. You must thin really hard if you are going to get any crop at all.

In winter, prune back 'spurs' on espalier-trained vines to one or two buds. On vines trained raspberry-fashion, cut out the old canes and untie the newly grown ones so that they hang from the main trunk. This looks untidy, but makes sure that when the buds break in the spring all the buds along the cane have equal vigour, instead of much of it going to a few at the end.

When the bunches are ripening under glass, keep the greenhouse vents open as much as possible when the weather is warm. If, as is often the case, the vines share a greenhouse with plants susceptible to red spider, such as peaches and nectarines, try to avoid getting any water on the grape bunches when hosing down the other fruit. If you do splash any fruit it is likely to rot.

Harvesting: Grapes will not be ripe until a week or more after the full colour has developed. Outside, wasps and birds will have become interested long before the fruit is sweet enough for you. Keep checking and deter pre-

dators with netting, either over the whole vine or bagged over individual bunches.

Under glass, the fruit can be left on the vine more or less until it is needed. The last bunches should still be good well into November if they were properly thinned, and if the greenhouse has been kept dry. Keep examining the bunches for split or mildewed fruit, and cut them out as soon as you see them, otherwise the rot will quickly spread. 'Black Hamburgh' hangs especially well, but 'Forster's Seedling' gets rather thick-skinned.

Pests and diseases: Scale insect, mealy bug, red spider and whitefly can all be a nuisance, though red spider is probably the most common. Try to get pest problems sorted out before the fruit begins to expand, as all sprays will damage the 'bloom'. Vine weevils can destroy plants grown in pots, though the grubs prefer the roots of many other greenhouse plants (especially primulas). Add soil pest killer to the potting compost, or water with spray-strength BHC.

Outdoors, wasps and birds will wreck the crop. Fruit bunches can be protected from both by bags of paper or fine netting. In this country, entire vineyards have to be completely netted.

Grey mould is common on ripening bunches, especially if these have not been thinned sufficiently. It is possible to spray, but it is better to examine the bunches regularly, and cut out infected fruit. Powdery mildew can attack leaves and fruit, most com-

monly in poorly ventilated greenhouses in cool summers. Do not plant grapes if you suspect that honey fungus is present in the soil.

WALNUT*

A stately and eventually very large (well over 18 m (60 ft) high) tree, the walnut is suitable only for sizeable gardens or parks. If you have the space, and can wait the twenty years it will take a young plant to produce nuts, then you should try it.

The walnut, native to North Asia, was known to the Greeks and the Romans, who dedicated it to Jupiter. It had innumerable medicinal uses, many of which survived into seventeenth-century Britain. Various parts of the plant were used against worms, both intestinal – walnuts were eaten at the start of a meal as a prophylactic – and earthworms – an infusion of walnut leaves discourages them in lawns too.

Cultivation: Walnuts are very deep rooting. This is useful in the garden, for it means that the trees can be underplanted. It also means that you should plant the smallest tree you can find, for large ones rarely establish themselves. Buy only grafted or

The walnut is a very fine and sizeable tree

budded plants; seedlings are very rarely satisfactory.

Walnuts will do well in a variety of soils, but prefer one that is deep and rich. They will give satisfactory crops well into Scotland.

Pests and diseases: Squirrels will steal the nuts if they can. If honey fungus strikes it can kill the tree quickly.

Harvesting: For pickling, harvest the fruits while they are still quite soft, and less than 3 cm (1¼ inches) long. Otherwise, leave them on the tree until October.

SOFT FRUITS

BLACKBERRY*

A familiar native, the blackberry is to be found in almost every hedgerow in Britain. Wild forms are very variable, however; they do not all have large fruit, and are not all prolific. While not denying the pleasures of berry-picking in the countryside, for heavy crops of large berries it is well worth having a few cultivated plants in the garden.

There are few varieties to choose from, only one or two which are suitable for small gardens. The least suitable is 'Himalaya', an enormously vigorous plant capable of producing several 6 m (20 ft) canes a season, each subsequently throwing out fruiting side branches up to a metre in length. Two better choices would be 'Oregon Thornless' and the parsley-leafed sort. The decorative leaves of both are attractively frilled and cut; the stems are thornless, which makes them much easier to prune, train and harvest. Both give good crops of richly flavoured berries. With canes of between 2 m (6 ft) and 3 m (10 ft) neither plant really needs all that much space.

Cultivation: The only feasible way of growing blackberries, especially the larger sorts, is on a wire framework of exactly the same sort as is used for espalier top fruit. The frame can be free-standing, or attached to a wall, but in either case needs to be big enough to accommodate two year's canes.

One wire supports canes from the right and left of each crown. There are various ways of doing this and for the small garden, system 2 (shown below) is probably the simplest to adopt.

Since the amount of fruit you get depends on the length of the canes grown the previous season, an annual mulch of manure is very beneficial.

If by chance you need more plants, or want to replace the ones you have, new crowns are easily produced. Simply let a cane or two grow so that its tip touches the soil and keep it in place with a stone

Three different systems of training blackberry canes

or a wire peg. It will soon take root. At the end of the season, detach the new plant.

Pests and diseases: Diseases are rare and the worst pests are, predictably, birds, which will take the fruits just before they are ripe. Not only could you lose most of the crop, but you could also have vigorous bramble seedlings appearing in every part of the garden, a major problem if you've planted 'Himalaya'. Grow blackberries in a fruit cage if possible to avoid this danger. Otherwise, use bird scarers. Trying to drape blackberry plants with netting is one of the least rewarding garden tasks, since so much of the fruit sticks through the mesh.

Raspberry beetle grubs can occasionally be a nuisance. If you find them one year, spray the flowering bushes the following year with Malathion or a derris-based spray. Work in the late evening when the bees are safely in the hive.

Harvesting: Fruit for eating fresh or for wine-making needs to be as sweet as possible, so leave it on the plant for as long as you can. Fruit for jams, jellies and pies is better if picked a little earlier when black in colour.

BLACKCURRANT*

Like the redcurrant, the blackcurrant is native to the woodlands of northern Europe, and a comparatively recent addition to the kitchen garden. It is a rich source of vitamin C. Its early uses were

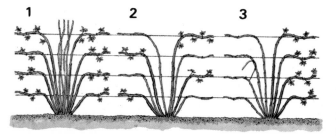

The blackberry hung with ripening fruit

largely medicinal but it is now used for desserts, jams, jellies, drinks and cordials. Children delight to eat fruit straight from the bush, though most adults prefer them cooked. The leaves, steeped in hot milk, give a delicate flavour to custards.

The bushes have a slightly different mode of growth to red and white currants, since they are less ready to spur, and do best in bush form in the fruit cage. It is possible to train them as fans against a wall, in which position they will fruit well, even when north-facing. Because this gives a correspondingly later crop, it was an early method

of extending the season.

There are a number of varieties available, none of which differ greatly from the wild plant. 'Baldwin' and 'Ben Lomond' are excellent for flavour. 'Wellington XXX' is a commonly seen mid-season plant, and 'Amos Black' is very late. Yield is sometimes improved by planting several varieties to ensure cross-pollination.

Cultivation: Blackcurrants do well in most soils, providing they are not waterlogged or bone dry. They will give fruit in cold gardens, and will also tolerate shade quite well in warmer ones.

Since fruiting is best on second-year wood, but less good on anything older, the gardener needs to ensure a continual production of strong new growth. Immediately after planting, cut back the stems to leave 5 cm (2 inches) of growth to encourage strong new side shoots. The prunings can be used as cuttings to raise new plants. Next season, cut out weak growths, which are unlikely to fruit, and give the plants a mulching.

Blackcurrants must be cut back immediately after planting

The ripe blackcurrant has an attractive bloom

When the bushes are mature, take out whole branches to let light and air into the centre of the bush. If you do not prune in this way the bush will become overgrown and unproductive, and it will be necessary to cut the whole bush back almost to ground level. This will encourage a mass of new growth; leave only the strongest 8-10 shoots to fruit the following season.

Where the bush is grown against a wall, tie in shoots to wires to make a fan. Mulch the root area to encourage growth. When the plant is mature, remove a spoke or two every year to ensure you get new shoots.

The bushes should be planted 2 m (6 ft) apart. This looks over-generous with new plants, or even semi-mature ones, but closer spacing makes harvesting impossible when bushes splay outwards loaded with fruit.

Pests and diseases: Big bud can be a nuisance in some gardens. In early spring, look for unusually large and swollen buds. Remove and burn them. Spray if necessary. Aphis, though, is the worst pest; if you fail to notice them or do not act against them, the plant's growth will be stunted, and the crop will fail both in the current year and the following one too.

Some varieties in some gardens get gooseberry mildew. Always keep a lookout as even a slight infection will ruin the crop. If your location is bad, and you do not have time to keep spraying, you should grow the variety 'Blackdown'.

Never use Lindex on blackcurrants.

Harvesting: It is easy to tell from the taste when blackcurrants are ready, but this can be a week or two after the berries have turned black. After full ripening, the berries can be left on the branches for a week or two without deteriorating too much if there is no time to harvest them.

If you can harvest the berries in peak condition, but want to store them for a while, pick the whole bunch by the stalk. Ideally the berries should be picked as soon as they are ripe and cooked soon afterwards. Remove them from the bush by picking them off the 'strig'.

BLUEBERRY**

Long popular in the United States, blueberries are building up a following in this country in areas with cool moist summers, and acid soils. 'High-bush' sorts are the ones most often seen here; they are branching leafy plants up to 1.5 m (5 ft) high, with heather-like flowers, and neat foliage that turns vivid red in autumn. The fruit is a delicious round and blue berry, heavily bloomed like a grape, and in some

varieties up to 2.5 cm (1 inch) in diameter. They are borne in sprays of 8-10 fruits.

Low-bush types, if you come across them, grow from creeping subterranean stems, and look rather like the British native whortleberry,

Blueberries can succeed well and are becoming popular

which belongs to the same genus as blueberry.

Of the great number of varieties available in the United States, only a few are offered here. These include 'Early Blue', 'Grover', 'Jersey' and 'Pemberton'. You will need to buy two sorts to ensure cross-pollination and a good yield.

Cultivation: If the soil in your area supports good ericas, azaleas and rhododendrons, which belong to the same family as the blueberry, it is probably suitable for this crop. Blueberries will do well on sandy or peaty soil, if the pH is between 4.3 and 4.8. As they also like high rainfall and cool summers with temperatures rarely above 21°C (70°F), they will generally do best in north-westerly parts of Britain.

In suitable areas, high-bush plants are spaced with their centres 1.2 m (4 ft) apart. On acid sandy soils, give an annual mulch of compost or rotted manure at a barrow-load for $3 m^2$ (4 yds^2). On peaty soil, an annual dressing of general fertilizer at 50 g/m^2 (2 oz/yd^2) will keep the plants cropping well.

Since blueberry bushes bear fruit on last season's wood, prune high-bush sorts lightly in the first few years, only taking out the weakest shoots. Later on, take out a few of the main branches each year, cutting them out at ground level to encourage strong new growth at the base. Each main shoot should only last for five or six years before it is pruned out. Low-bush sorts should be cut back to ground level every three or four years to encourage the 'rhizome' to throw up new shoots.

Blueberries are easy to propagate by taking cuttings in very early spring before the buds begin to expand. The cuttings should be about 20 cm (8 inches) long. Rub out any flower buds. Insert the cuttings into sandy, moist

soil in frames. Move the rooted plants to their final positions in the following autumn.

Pests and diseases: In the United States blueberries are susceptible to many serious pests and diseases; as they have not long been in wide-spread cultivation in this country, however, problems are few; birds adore the berries, so it is essential to net the plants.

Harvesting: Depending on variety, fruit ripens from mid-July, when the full blue colour has developed.

GOOSEBERRY*

Gooseberry bushes, small to medium in size are somehow redolent of cottage and kitchen gardens of the past. The fruit is immensely variable – early or late, smooth or hairy, sweet or sour, soft or crisp (some sorts were used as salads in Elizabethan England) – and it comes in all sorts of colours including green, yellow, red, white and, no longer to be seen, black. They all make delicious desserts, jams, jellies and wines, and the sweet sorts are lovely eaten straight from the garden. Since dessert fruits do not travel well, they are less often seen at the greengrocer.

The bushes make good hedges as most plants are quite spiny. They look attractive in the fruit cage or are easily trained against walls, where they are happy to face in any direction. The dessert types are an exception to this as they need plenty of direct sunlight. All kinds are easily trained as cordons or fans. Even neglected plants fruit

Gooseberries take on a translucent quality when ripe

quite well, though they eventually become badly tangled and need savage thinning out every couple of years.

There were once enormous numbers of gooseberry varieties. In the nineteenth century gooseberry clubs raised hundreds of varieties from seed, many of which are still to be found. See what is available locally. Of the well-known ones, 'Green Gem', 'Lord Derby' (red) and 'Leveller' (yellow) are excellent in flavour. Bullfinches like the buds of 'Leveller'. 'Leveller' and 'Lord Derby' are susceptible to mildew, but do not like sulphur-based sprays, so use benomyl instead. 'Lancashire Lad' is resistant to mildew.

Cultivation: Gooseberries are

ground. They should root fairly easily, and next autumn when you move them to where they are to fruit, rub out the shoots and buds that were below ground level. The idea is to provide a short bud-free 'neck' for the new bush.

Pests and diseases: Birds are the worst menace; bullfinches peck out young buds in early spring and several species attack swelling fruits later in the season. If bullfinches are a major nuisance for you, wind skeins of black thread around the twigs, though the thread itself can be a nuisance later in the season. Bushes with maturing fruits can generally be protected with flapping strips of plastic. For dessert gooseberries, growing in a fruit cage is the best answer.

Gooseberry sawfly and magpie moth caterpillars can also be a major hazard. In late May and early June, look closely at the leaves, particularly those in the centre of the bush. Caterpillars strip away the leaf blade, leaving the main veins. Whole areas of a bush can be quickly stripped, so act fast. Most insecticides are suitable.

Aphids can also be a problem; keep a check on young leaves. If they look curiously curled, have a look underneath. A winter spray should reduce the problem but if it is not effective you may have to spray again in summer.

Gooseberry mildew often goes unnoticed early in the season, only to reveal itself later and ruin the crop. In plants grown against a wall make sure that the leaves and fruits farthest from the light

fairly undemanding; they do well in most soils, but prefer well-drained loam. An annual mulch of manure or compost is helpful, and keeps down weeds. Potash deficiency can show up as scorched leaf margins; use a potash-rich fertilizer, or carefully fork in a small quantity of sulphate of potash. A handfork is best for this since it will not damage the roots. Less than 28 g (1 oz) will suit a well-grown bush.

Gooseberries will fruit quite well with no attention at all, though you will get a much higher yield if you find time to prune. Cut back the main growth shoots of young bushes by half each winter to encourage strong new growth. Varieties with a drooping habit of growth should be cut back to an upward-facing bud.

Clear out weak and twiggy growth that will not bear much fruit.

As the structure of the bush develops, encourage formation of fruiting spurs by cutting back laterals to 7.5 cm (3 inches). In summer, shorten laterals so that they have 5 leaves left.

Gooseberries make good single, double or triple cordons. Allow the leader or leaders to grow unchecked until they are as tall as you need. Winter-prune laterals to 3 buds, and in summer prune to 5 leaves.

Once you have found a variety that suits you, it is easily propagated from cuttings. In autumn, take shoots of the summer's growth about 20-30 cm (8 to 12 inches) long. Plant them in a shady place so that only the topmost three or four buds are above are free of the characteristic white fur that turns black. If you manage to catch the plant at this stage – generally just after the fruit begins to swell – and arrest the infection, strip off the blemished fruit. If you remove them early, the uninfected fruit remaining on the bush will swell to a greater size, so the overall yield will not be much reduced.

Harvesting: Once the berries have swollen to a reasonable size they can be picked for jams, jellies, and sauces for mackerel or goose. They do not have to be harvested all at once. Those left on the bushes will ripen until they split. Bushes outside cages will be the subject of eager attention from birds as soon as the fruit starts ripening.

Undamaged berries can be kept for a short time in the refrigerator.

LOGANBERRY, TAYBERRY AND BOYSENBERRY*

A number of species in the genus *Rubus*, both American and European, can be crossed with each other. The hybrids are all fairly modern, the loganberry and boysenberry having arisen this century in the USA. They are crosses between the raspberry and a sort of blackberry. The tayberry is a new Scottish hybrid, very mild in taste and quite similar in shape to the loganberry.

The hybrid berries all crop exceptionally well, which is the main reason for their success. Some loganberry stocks no longer crop well, however, and you will need to buy 'LY59' or 'LY54' to get

a good yield. The thornless hybrids are useful.

The fresh berries are colourful, sweet, and abundant. They can be made into very good jams and jellies.

Cultivation: As might be expected, the culture of these hybrids resembles that of both parents. Since the canes are generally between 2 and 2.4 m (6 and 8 ft) long, they can be trained up or along wires depending on the amount of space available.

Pests and diseases: They are the same as for raspberry (see below) and blackberry (page 56).

Harvesting: Pick the fruit when the full colour has formed. Ripe berries are easily crushed, so go carefully.

RASPBERRY*

The raspberry is native to the woodlands and fields of Europe, particularly its northern parts. The cultivated raspberry seems to have lost a little of the subtle flavour of its wild ancestor, though they yield heavily, are sweeter, and can be grown close to the kitchen door.

Well-grown rows, neatly tied and weighed down with lovely soft red fruit, look wonderful in the kitchen garden. Good dessert varieties are 'Glen Clova', 'Malling Jewel' and the late ripening 'Malling Admiral'. If you like unusual-looking fruit, try growing some of the yellow fruited sorts. They have also a subtly different flavour.

Autumn-fruiting varieties extend the season in favoured districts. The flavour is slightly inferior to the summer-fruiting varieties.

Cultivation: The rootstock throws up shoots from below ground. They last two years; in the first they make growth, in the second they bear fruit. New roots or crowns are planted 45 cm (18 inches) apart, with about 2 m (6 ft) between the rows if you have more than one. New canes are tied to a wire or string framework, either free-standing or against a wall. The simplest way of keeping the

canes upright is to insert a 2.1 m (7 ft) bamboo cane every 2 m (6 ft) or so with horizontal strings 1 m (3 ft) above ground level and, when the new growth needs more support, at 2 m (6 ft) above that again.

If the canes outgrow the

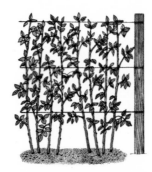

RIGHT: *A simple support system for raspberry canes*
BELOW: *Raspberries are a very popular fruiting crop*

wires or strings, simply cut them off, or tie them into the topmost support. Do not let them grow through the fruit cage roof.

Dig out new shoots that interfere with the pathway between the rows of canes. As soon as fruiting has finished, cut out spent canes to give plenty of room and light to the new ones.

The autumn fruiting sorts are treated in another way. They fruit on canes grown earlier in the same season. Fruiting stops in late autumn and the canes are cut down to within a few inches of the ground in February. The rootstocks tend to produce very large numbers of new shoots each spring, so be ruthless and dig up those that will get in your way.

All raspberries appreciate an annual mulch of compost, manure, or peat and artificial fertilizer. In either case, keep the plants well watered, especially as the fruit is swelling.

Pests and diseases: Aphis show up first. Keep checking the undersides of the leaves at the top of new canes. Raspberry beetles are a major nuisance, the grubs feeding on the base of each ripening berry, and are often found curled up inside when the fruit is picked. They can eventually ruin the entire crop. Spray the fruit when the first berries begin to colour.

Various fungus diseases can affect canes and spurs. None is common, and all are easily eradicated. Virus diseases, transmitted by both aphis and eelworm, are common and ineradicable. The leaves become mottled and

yellow, often distorted in shape, and the plants eventually stop fruiting. Burn the entire plant, and replant virus-free stock in fresh ground.

Raspberries are so attractive to birds that you will be very lucky if you can harvest a respectable crop on canes grown outside a fruit cage.

Harvesting: Pick the fruit when it is fully coloured. Use the sharper tasting varieties for jam or in a splendid summer pudding with some of the other red berries.

REDCURRANT AND WHITECURRANT*

These pretty bushes with attractive leaves have branches hung with trails of small yellowish flowers in late spring, and in high summer with lovely translucent berries, in shades of ruby, garnet, or palest milky amber. The species is native to North West Europe, and does not seem to have been cultivated until the sixteenth century. By nature a woodland plant,

A bunch of ripe red currants

it is not surprising that it will grow and fruit well in light shade. It was once thought that bushes in such a position gave tastier fruit.

Redcurrants, apart from marvellous jelly and jam, also make good garnishes, especially for roast hare, or the first pheasants of the season. They were once crystallized for use in the winter. 'Red Lake' and 'White Grape' both have excellent flavours. Whitecurrants also make a good wine.

Cultivation: Young plants to be grown as bushes are set 2 m (6 ft) apart. Single cordons should be 60 cm-1 m (2-3 ft) apart, doubles and triples 1.2-1.5 m (4-5 ft) apart. Neither sort is fussy about soil type, but they like regular annual mulches of compost or manure.

Pruning is not difficult. Against a wall, especially a stone one, you will find that the plants have a natural inclination to keep to the surface. This helps if you do not have much time for pruning. They are easily made into fans and cordons. Select the main growth shoots, and induce spurs by summer pruning the lateral shoots back to five leaves; winter prune back to two buds. Reduce the leaders or main branches on a bush, by about half of the season's growth each autumn, or back to a bud or two if the plant has filled the available space.

The plants like a potash-rich diet. Add a small handful of sulphate of potash for each square yard of soil, or dress with ash from the bonfire, or the grate if you burn wood.

Pests and diseases: Fortunately, red- and white-currants suffer from few diseases, and none of these is dangerous. However, birds and aphis will rob you of your crop if left alone. Bushes need to be in a cage, and cordons need netting as soon as the fruit begins to colour. Unpointed, stone walls will harbour mice who will also garner the berries.

Keep a constant watch for aphis, checking the under-surface of young leaves. If they are curled or distorted, you will probably find that they are thick with insects. Spray liberally, or remove the leaves.

Harvesting: Can take place as soon as the strings of berries have taken colour. White-currants become pinkish and translucent; keep tasting to check for ripeness. The berries will hang in good condition for several weeks if you have gluts of other fruit keeping the cook busy with the jam pan.

RHUBARB*

The familiar denizen of neglected gardens and allotments, the rhubarb is a handsome and generous provider of the earliest fresh desserts of the year. It was first grown here in the sixteenth century in error, having been taken for another species that had important medicinal uses. Only the roots were used for their laxative property, until the eighteenth century, when

Rhubarb is a very popular crop, being easy to grow and prolific. It can also be forced to provide some early fruit

the French discovered that the leaf stalks were delicious, and had no evil effects on the digestion.

Rhubarb seeds prolifically, and there are many varieties in cultivation. There is not an enormous difference between them, but 'Champagne' and 'Early Albert' are good. Virus-free stocks have been produced, but, ironically, have little flavour.

Cultivation: Rhubarb grows in most types of soil, and in spite of neglect. However, it is best in good deep soil, with plenty of feeding. If you have a compost heap, plant rhubarb nearby and you will get giant plants.

When it is doing well, rhubarb tries to flower. The spikes are very striking, but it is best to break them off at ground level. Plant new crowns in autumn 1 m (3 ft) apart. Do not harvest any stems the following season, and only a few the next. This allows the crown to build up its vigour. Three or four plants are enough for most families. The first few spring croppings are particularly delicious and very welcome at a time when other fruit in the garden is not productive.

Rhubarb can be forced if you want something fresh once the last of the apples and pears have been used up by March. Put a black plastic bucket over a vigorous crown, and pile manure round the outside to warm the interior. Alternatively, dig the crown up, prop it up with soil or moist peat in the bottom of a plastic sack, and take it indoors. Store somewhere with slight warmth

with the bag closed. After a few weeks there will be some nice blanched shoots.

After forcing, the crowns need a rest. Feed them up with mulches of compost or rotted manure, or water them fortnightly with liquid fertilizer. Take no more stalks for the year. If you need the space, discard them and plant new crowns next season.

Pests and diseases: None.

Harvesting: Let the young leaf stalks reach a reasonable length before you pick them. Stalks that still have plenty of growth to make seem to retain the laxative properties of the root. It is always recommended that leaf stalks should be pulled off rather than cut, but cutting does not seem to damage the plants. Do not eat any of the green leafy part; it is poisonous.

STRAWBERRY*

Almost everyone likes strawberries, an easily grown fruit that speedily produces a crop, and is easily propagated and maintained.

The large sorts now so widely grown are almost all hybrids between various American species. They started appearing in the mid-1700s, and are still the consuming passion of plant

RIGHT: The strawberry in fruit and flower

breeders. New varieties are bred for colour, size, marketability, season of fruiting and disease resistance – not always for flavour. Do not be persuaded to buy the latest variety by enthusiastic publicity. Buy or beg a few plants of as many varieties as you can, and see which you like best. There are great variations in flavour. Use only obviously healthy plants, the leaves of which are unblemished and well-coloured. Although the oldest varieties are immune to most virus diseases, modern ones often are not, and infection may spread to any susceptible varieties already planted.

Cultivation: Having settled on the variety or varieties you want, find out if virus-tested stocks are available. Rooted runners can be planted in the garden at any time of year. Runners planted by July, however, can be cropped the following summer; those planted later than August should be given a year to

BELOW: Plant strawberries so the crown is level with the soil
RIGHT: Superfluous strawberry runners should be removed

build up a strong crown. To do this, remove the flowering shoots as soon as they appear.

Modern strawberries should, in the first instance, be planted 38 cm (15 inches) apart, in rows 75 cm (2 ft 6 inches) apart. This gives plenty of space for maintenance, feeding, spreading out the developing sprays of fruit and harvesting.

In ideal circumstances – that is, if the gardener has plenty of time – all runners should be removed during the growing season, unless you want to increase the number of plants. This leaves the strawberries in neat rows, and certainly makes life easier. In many gardens, however, the strawberry patch is allowed to become a jungle of new plants. If the ground was in good shape when the bed was formed, such tangles can be extremely fruitful for the next two seasons or so. After that, pests generally build up, especially if the dead leaves are not removed each winter, and the plants become starved. You should then root as many runners as you need to re-start the bed. Clear out the old plants completely at the end of the second or third crop. Manure the ground, add a handful of potash for each square yard of ground, and replant.

If you have time to keep the strawberries in neat rows, lightly mulch between the rows in early spring, using compost or rotted manure. Use about a spadeful for each crown, spreading carefully to avoid burying the leaves and growth points. Replace the old plants with young ones every three or four years.

Plants grown in rows can also enjoy the luxury of having the sprays of fruit placed on straw or even special fibre mats, to keep them clean and less susceptible to disease: this is worth doing if you want top quality fruit.

There are early, mid- and late-maturing strawberries. It is possible to speed up the production of any of them by using cloches. Glass ones give the earliest crop of all, but plastic ones, even if just of polythene sheeting, can be quite effective. Put the cloches in place as the days begin to lengthen. Once the flowers are open allow plenty of air to circulate, especially on warm days. The flowers need full pollination if the fruit is to develop evenly, and if the cloches are closed the insects will not be able to get in to do their work. Later on, as the fruit swells, it is equally important to keep the cloches ventilated to prevent rot.

In the greenhouse, simply plant strawberries in open beds, or pot up vigorous plants in autumn. Keep a watch for aphids. Some sprays, for example, malathion, seem to damage young leaves and flowers.

A large pot of strawberries can look attractive on a patio. Strawberry barrels and other complex devices for growing tiers of fruit can be tricky to manage. Seepage can saturate the lowest part of the soil while leaving the topmost part bone dry.

In the interests of having strawberries over a long period, you may decide to grow types which produce fruits throughout summer and early autumn, although the yields are not enormous at any one time. Children like them, though many adults will prefer the flavour of single-flush strawberries like 'Cambridge Rival', 'Royal Sovereign', 'Talisman', and 'Cambridge Late Pine'.

Pests and diseases: The main pest, aphids, distributes virus disease as well as distorting the new leaves. Aphids appear in early spring and as they tend to stay close to the centre of the crowns, their presence is often shown only by these distortions. Keep checking, and spray if this becomes necessary.

Virus disease shows up as leaf blotching, or mottling in purple and yellow, as leaf distortions and lack of flowers. Burn the plants and get virus-free stocks which should be planted in another site.

Beetles and slugs can ruin ripe berries. Clear away dead leaves in autumn to give them less cover. Both beetles and slugs can be controlled by using methiocarb pellets. Birds are of course a major hazard and there is little point in growing strawberries if you cannot provide adequate protection.

In some seasons, ripening fruits develop brown patches which are soon covered in grey mould (dense masses of spores). The spread of the disease can be halted by most garden fungicides. Do not, however, use thiram or captan on fruits that will be eaten fresh. If possible, remove all infected fruit before spores appear. Next year, spray with Benomyl two or three times at 10-day intervals once flowering has started.

Harvesting: The large fruit that ripens first is known as the 'king' and should be picked as soon as it turns a good red colour. The other berries ripen quickly thereafter so check the bed every day. Ripe fruit will store for several days if chilled.

ALPINE STRAWBERRIES
Alpine strawberries have developed from the common European wild strawberry and have been admired since Roman times. The small fruits are slightly fiddly to pick, but

Tiny alpine strawberries

the flavour is marvellous.

The plants are usually runnerless, and are propagated by seed, or by teasing apart mature plants. To grow from seed, simply scrape some seeds from a ripe fruit and sow them at once in soil-based compost in a 10 cm (4 inch) pot. Seed will germinate in two weeks or so. If you have sown seed in July or August, the seedlings will be big enough to prick out directly into the garden next spring. Space them 25-30 cm (10-12 inches) apart, with 45 cm (18 inches) between the rows. The plants should be in fruit by early July. If you sow in spring, you should have some fruit by the autumn. Protect the ripening fruit from greedy birds with flapping plastic strips.

Several varieties are available. 'Baron Solemacher' is recommended; 'Reines des Vallées' is superb. Particularly delicious are the white- or green-fruited ones, creamy, fragrant and full of flavour.

MUSK STRAWBERRY

Gourmets regard this European species as the finest strawberry. With deep red, round fruits, they look quite different and their taste is really sumptuous.

Male and female plants are needed. Both sorts runner strongly and soon form an impenetrable and productive patch. Throughout the growing season birds will be attracted to them. For this reason they should be grown beneath the protection of nets if you want any fruits.

UNUSUAL AND EXOTIC FRUITS

CITRUS FRUITS**/***
(including lemon, orange,
grapefruit)

Exceptional bushes or trees, the plants of the citrus family have glossy leaves, white, heavily perfumed flowers and colourful fruits. All of them can be grown with the help of a greenhouse or sun-room. With the exception of the grapefruit and tangerine, which are both nineteenth-century introductions, they have been grown here since the earliest seventeenth century, and have often yielded vast crops. One eighteenth-century garden often pro-duced more than 10,000 oranges a year.

Most gardeners and most children will have sown seeds of a breakfast grapefruit or Christmas tangerine. Seeds of all citrus fruits ger-minate easily; most people select the vigorous ones, and are delighted with their rapid growth. However, it is usual-ly best to look after the least vigorous plants, as these are most likely to resemble the parent plant and give good fruit. The vigorous seedlings will be hybrid, and more often than not will produce poor fruit.

Young plants have spiny branches, but as they begin to mature, ten or more years later, the growth is less armoured. The first flowers are always an excitement, and even one will scent the whole greenhouse.

Buy named varieties of cit-rus plants from a reputable nursery or garden centre.

A colourful crop of ripe lemons

These will have been raised from cuttings or grafts from mature plants, and will fruit quite soon. Lemons need a 30 cm (12 inch) pot. Oranges and grapefruits need tubs. The lemon 'Imperial' is excellent, and there is a good grapefruit called 'Forster's'. The type of tangerine called 'Satsuma' is prolific and fairly hardy. Do not despise the small 'oranges' found on tiny bushes at the florist's. These are calamondins, easy to grow, and if you can keep it going, a large bush can look very glamorous indeed. Stew the fruit whole in syrup, and serve warm or chilled with plenty of whipped cream.

Cultivation: Use a soil-based compost in pot or tub. An Italian pot of moulded terracotta is best. All citrus fruits like a reasonable temperature for growth. They will grow quite well out of doors in sheltered parts of southern England, but need to be under glass all year in the north, and certainly in all parts of Scotland.

Water should be given carefully. If the plants dry out, or become waterlogged, new leaves will be shed and all the growth points will drop. If feeding with liquid fertilizer, use at half the recommended

Grown under glass citrus fruits, like this orange, can crop well

strength. Over-enthusiastic feeding, as well as some insecticides, can also cause leaf-drop.

Beneath glass, try to keep plants lightly shaded. If flowers form, rejoice and be thankful. Young fruits will take 6-18 months to ripen.

In autumn, bring outdoor plants inside. Most citrus are happy in winter temperatures of about 4°C (40°F), and some oranges and grapefruits will tolerate temperatures a few degrees below freezing. If you do not have a green-

71

house, even a light room, corridor or porch can perfectly well be used as an 'orangery'.

Pruning is only a matter of keeping the plants fairly open, both for light, and ease of pest control. If you do not mind waiting longer than usual for fruit, train your plants as standards, which look very handsome.

Pests and diseases: In this country, diseases are few. The worst pests are scale insects and red spider. Scale insects will reveal themselves as black powdery spots on the leaves, which is actually fungus growing on the sticky secretions emitted by insects feeding on leaves higher up. Have a look on the undersides of leaves for brown waxy-looking scales clustered along the leaf mid-ribs. Spray with malathion. Keep checking; a bad attack of scale renders plants very unsightly, and will eventually kill them.

Red spider goes for young leaves, particularly of lemon trees. Spray, or hose down.

Harvesting: After it reaches full colour leave the fruit for as long as you can to ripen on the tree, where it looks highly decorative.

KIWI**

The kiwi, or Chinese gooseberry, is a very attractive climbing fruit with remarkable leaves, which are at first covered with dense scarlet hairs, maturing to yellowish green. The leaf stalks and stems retain their colourful bristles throughout the growing season.

The plants are best attached to a framework of wires on a south-facing wall. Kiwis are easily grown from seed, but as male and female plants are needed if you are to get fruit, a number of plants must be grown to maturity to ensure that you have both sexes. Plants will take four to five years to flower. If you do not want to wait that long, buy in sexed plants from a nursery.

The flowers, of white or cream, are pleasantly scented; the fruits that follow are brown, densely bristled and oblong. The flesh inside is a clear fresh green; the numerous small black pips are edible.

Kiwi plants with attractively variegated leaves are grown for foliage only, and do not give good fruit.

Cultivation: Since the Kiwi is fairly new to British gardens, little is known of its likes and hates. It seems to do well in any good garden soil, and crops liberally out of doors well into Northumberland.

Pests and diseases: None.

Harvesting: Pick the fruit as soon as it yields to slight pressure.

MELON***

The melon is a gorgeous fruit, particularly so when still warm from the sun of your own garden. It will not be a surprise to learn that such perfection calls for a certain amount of fuss and some hard work.

Innumerable varieties are available. If you find something you like, keep a few seeds, for they will almost certainly come true. Alternatively, try some of the 'Ogen' types, or 'Blenheim Orange'.

Some varieties claim resistance to disease, but this cannot always be relied upon.

Cultivation: Sow the seeds in gentle warmth, in late April, or early May in a propagator or airing cupboard if at 18-20°C (65-70°F). Put them singly in small pots. The seedlings dislike root damage, and will not recover if you tear a group of seedlings apart after several have germinated in one pot. After germination, grow the seedlings on in the greenhouse or a sunny win-

dowsill until late May. Plant out in frames, in greenhouse beds, in large pots, in growing bags or, in the warmest parts of the country, in the open ground to be grown as 'cordons' under cloches. One plant eventually takes up 3-5 m^2 (4-6 yds^2).

Under glass, train the plants up strings. If you leave them on the flat, you will not be able to hose off red spider, a pest which is rather less likely to attack in frames.

On strings, prune side shoots back to two leaves, or if there is a female flower on the shoot, to two or three leaves beyond the flower. In a frame, pinch out the growing point of the main shoot once there are 6-8 leaves, to encourage branching.

Once flowers are open, look for males, which have a boss of stripy anthers in the middle, and no fruitlet below,

Melons will sometimes need to be netted for support as the fruits ripen and grow heavy

and females, with a wavy style in the middle, and a potential fruitlet beneath the flower. On a warm dry day, fertilize the females by picking a male, stripping off the petals, and pushing the anthers into the female.

Neither sort of flower lasts much more than a day, or a bit longer, so check the plant regularly. If it is producing only male flowers, wait for the warmer weather which produces females.

After fertilization, the young fruitlets soon start swelling. On strings, small-fruited varieties do not really need support, but if the variety produces large melons, you will need a small square of netting left over from the fruit cage, and some string, to rig up a support.

In frame-grown plants, make sure that plenty of sun reaches the young fruit. Strip away any leaves that shade them. As the fruit grows, place it on a tile or broad flat stone. This gives a little extra warmth, and keeps the fruit off damp soil. Turn the fruit round every few days to ensure even ripening.

Pests and diseases: Various wilts and mildews can inflict major damage. Spray all plants regularly with fungicide. If whole plants suddenly collapse and you find blackish or brownish swellings just above the roots, throw the plant out and start again, preferably with new soil.

Red spider is a constant menace. Keep spraying, or hose down regularly – the leaves are quite tough. If you do not do either for a while, the plant will be ruined in ten days. Whitefly can also be a bit of a nuisance.

Slugs will be eager to eat into ripening fruits, especially if you have not put tiles under them. Use proprietary slug bait.

Harvesting: When the melons begin to turn yellow, and to smell delicious, you will be tempted to eat them, but wait for another day or two. If you have harvested too soon, leave the fruit in a warm and sunny place until the flesh by the stalk end feels soft to the touch.

Melons stay at their peak for a few days, but you should not, in any circumstances eat one that has gone 'over the top'. They can make you quite ill.

At the end of the season you will be left with a number of unripe fruit. They make excellent chutney.

PASSION FRUIT**

Various sorts of passion fruit are grown, some for their fruit, others for their pharmacological properties. The passion of their title refers to the Christian event; the flowers were thought to show religious symbolism.

The usual dessert sort is only marginally hardy outdoors in this country; it will probably not survive a harsh winter. The remarkable flowers are of a soft cream colour, and have a perfume, which is sharp and rather enticing.

Where the plants are grown under glass, ripe fruit can be had from the earliest flowers, though they are rarely as delicious as those imported from America or southern Europe. Neverthe-

less this is a plant worth growing for the certainty of the extraordinary flowers, and the possibility of fruits.

Cultivation: Passion fruit plants grown outdoors must be against a south-facing wall; any good garden soil will do. Give them some overwinter protection if possible, even if this means pulling the shoots from the supporting framework of wires, bunching them together, and wrapping them with straw. Since the flowers come on mature new growth, if all last year's has been killed off, you will only have flowers by September, and there will not be time for the fruit to ripen before the short days of winter.

For plants grown in pots, use a soil-based compost and train them up a pyramid of canes. Keep very well fed with liquid fertilizer. Undernourished plants will not produce flowers. If you are planting them out in greenhouse beds, grow them up a trellis.

Pests and diseases: Generally trouble-free.

Harvesting: If you are lucky enough to have fruits, pick them as they begin to blacken and wrinkle. Cut them in half, and eat the lovely contents with a small spoon, ignoring the seeds.

PINEAPPLE***

The pineapple is as sumptuous in appearance as it is in flavour, and home-grown ones can be very fine. Before they began to be imported from the Caribbean in the early nineteenth century, huge quantities were grown

in British greenhouses. They are not at all difficult, and although few modern gardeners could afford to produce pineapples throughout the year, it is fun to have a few plants under glass.

The choice of variety is dictated by whatever is sold by your greengrocer.

Cultivation: Buy a nice-looking pineapple with a fresh and well-developed crown of leaves. It does not matter if this has been 'treated' and contains a yellow plastic stopper. Slice off the crown where it joins the fruit. Dust the cut with flowers of sulphur to prevent rot. Leave the crown in an airy sheltered place for two or three days so that the cut dries.

Put the crown in a propagator, in gritty and free-draining soil, to make roots. 'Treated' crowns should throw out several side shoots. These often have embryonic roots at their bases, so simply detach them and plant them up. The treatment you give rooted plants depends on the winter temperature you can offer. If this does not exceed 4°C (40°F), put the plant in a 25 cm (10 inch) pot filled with very rich compost but with a gritty and free-draining soil around the neck of the plant. Horticultural grit is ideal. At low temperatures damp soil around the neck could lead to rot in the fruit.

If you can offer them 13-16°C (55-60°F) pineapples will keep growing all winter with less risk of rot. Plant them in

The pineapple, grown under glass, is a sumptuous and exotic crop with its unusual fruits

compost enriched with well-rotted manure. You should be able to harvest the first fruit 12-18 months after rooting a crown.

Although pineapples will grow on a sunny windowsill, they are unlikely to fruit in that situation. A greenhouse or south-facing conservatory is much better. Expert growers used to be able to produce fruits weighing 1 kilo (2 lbs) or more.

Pests and diseases: The ever-present danger of neck rot can sometimes be kept at bay by the fungicides, though they will not compensate for poor growing conditions. Scale insects and mealy bugs can be a menace. Keep checking the foliage if either pest is to be found in your greenhouse, and spray with malathion if necessary.

Harvesting: Pick the fruits when they begin to smell good. It is better to harvest them when slightly under-ripe, and store them. The fruits lose their flavour if they ripen fully on the plant. Traditionally, they were harvested with several inches of stem – enough for the footman to hold while he cut you a slice – and the crowns were always returned to the kitchen garden.

POMEGRANATE**

An ancient and magical crop, grown since prehistoric times in the Middle and Near East, the pomegranate played a part in Greek and Roman mythology, which was perhaps one of its attractions for some classically educated British gardeners of the seventeenth century.

Seed is widely available, and if you have space against a south-facing wall, the plant is well worth growing for its lovely flowers. The bushes are perfectly hardy even well into Scotland.

The leaves are narrow and numerous, and are held on slender pinkish stems. The flowers are extraordinary, sometimes 4 cm (1½ inches) across, of an intense vermilion, with petals as crumpled and insubstantial as those of a poppy. There were once pink-white and striped sorts

available, but these seem to have vanished.

In warm situations out of doors, the fruit expands well enough, but rarely sweetens sufficiently to eat. It will, however, ripen in a heated greenhouse or sunroom. As the plants do well in tubs or large pots, this is the best place for them. The fruit lasts over winter on the branch, ripening in early summer. Large plants hanging with amber-pink fruits and brilliant flowers are a really magnificent sight.

ture plants so if possible buy commercially propagated material.

Pests and diseases: None in this country.

Harvesting: Fully ripened fruits split, showing the translucent pink interior through the burnished skin.

SUGAR CHERRY

There are a number of edible members of this genus, which includes the decorative varieties such as the familiar red 'Chinese Lantern'. The edible variety usually cultivated is *Physalis edulis*, an easily grown annual. It produces papery husks, greeny-yellow in colour, containing a soft yellow berry with a subtle and distinctive flavour. Since yields are not high, the plant should be seen more as a novelty than a serious crop.

Cultivation: In good conditions the plant will produce masses of foliage and little fruit, so prick out seedlings, one to a 11 cm (4½ inch) pot. At least a dozen or so will be needed. Place them in a greenhouse or frame, and grow on until fruit ripens. Tomato fertilizer should be given twice a week.

Pests and diseases: Red spider and greenfly can be a nuisance. Woodlice will damage the fruit casing.

Harvesting: It is easy to inspect the fruit inside each husk. Do not pick them until they are rich yellow. The whole husk should separate easily from the plant. The flavour will improve if you leave both husk and fruit on a sunny shelf for another week or two; in fact they will keep for months.

If you do not have room for the trees which eventually result, grow the charming dwarf pomegranate. This will flower and fruit in an 11 cm (4½ inch) pot, but the lovely fruits are not edible.

Cultivation: Outdoors, pomegranates like deep well-drained soil. Feed with bonemeal and potash. Manure or compost encourages vegetation at the expense of flowers.

Pomegranate plants are a mass of tiny branches which are difficult to prune. As

The pomegranate is a very beautiful bush which produces magnificent flowers

major branches develop, tie them back to the wall. The plants will eventually make very handsome and informal wall plants. If you have a warm house wall to give them, they will fill a whole gable. The plants are self-fertile.

Seedlings take some time to mature, but fruiting is much faster on plants taken as cuttings from already ma-

INDEX

ACKNOWLEDGEMENTS

The following photographs were taken specially for
Octopus Books Ltd: Michael Boys 5, 36-7, 39, 65, 67;
Jerry Harpur 2, 7, 32, 38, 43, 47, 49, 58, 60-1, 62-3;
Neil Holmes 13, 33, 35, 40-1, 46, 50, 53, 59, 69, 72-3,
76-7, 80; George Wright 1, 51, 64.

The publishers would like to thank the following
individuals and organisations for their kind
permission to reproduce the photographs in this
book: A-Z Botanical Collection 31; Heather Angel/
Biofotos 75; Brian Furner Collection 23, 25; Harry
Smith Horticultural Photographic Collection 34, 45,
55, 57, 70, 71.

Illustrations by Christine Davison of The Garden
Studio.